Lone Star Spooks

Searching for Ghosts in Texas

Nate Riddle

Schiffer Publishing Ltd

30 Lower Valley Road, Atglen, Pennsylvania 19310

Schiffer Books are available at special discounts for bulk purchases for sales promotions or premiums. Special editions, including personalized covers, corporate imprints, and excerpts can be created in large quantities for special needs. For more information contact the publisher:

Published by Schiffer Publishing Ltd.
4880 Lower Valley Road
Atglen, PA 19310
Phone: (610) 593-1777; Fax: (610) 593-2002
E-mail: Info@schifferbooks.com

For the largest selection of fine reference books on this and related subjects,
please visit our website at: **www.schifferbooks.com**
We are always looking for people to write books on new and related subjects.
If you have an idea for a book please contact us at the above address.

This book may be purchased from the publisher.
Include $5.00 for shipping.
Please try your bookstore first.
You may write for a free catalog.

In Europe, Schiffer books are distributed by
Bushwood Books
6 Marksbury Ave.
Kew Gardens
Surrey TW9 4JF England
Phone: 44 (0) 20 8392 8585; Fax: 44 (0) 20 8392 9876
E-mail: info@bushwoodbooks.co.uk
Website: www.bushwoodbooks.co.uk

Other Schiffer Books on Related Subjects:
Texas Ghosts: Galveston, Houston, and Vicinity, 978-0-7643-3410-8, $14.99
Ghosts of San Antonio, 978-0-7643-3122-0, $14.99
Spirits of Dallas: The Haunting of the Big D, 978-0-7643-3036-0, $14.99
Ghosts of Fort Worth: Investigating Cowtown's Most Haunted Locations, 978-0-7643-2813-8,$14.95
Haunted Austin, Texas, 978-0-7643-3298-2, $14.99
Supernatural Texas: A Field Guide, 978-0-7643-3309-5, $24.99

Designed by Mark David Bowyer
Type set in A Charming Font Superexpanded / NewBaskerville BT

ISBN: 978-0-7643-3744-4
Printed in the United States of America

Contents

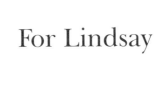
For Lindsay

Acknowledgments

There are honestly too many people to thank in such a small space, but I'll give it a whirl anyway! I'd like to first thank Schiffer Publishing and my amazing editors Dinah Roseberry and Jennifer Marie Savage for taking a chance on this book.

To Nick and Mitch, thanks for telling me to just go for it. To my amazingly supportive family and friends of which I'm lucky enough to have too many to list here, thanks for your undying support. To my awesome wife Lindsay, thanks so much for patiently listening to my endless ramblings about ghosts on an almost nightly basis for over a year. To Leia, our beloved Beagle, thanks for not eating the final manuscript.

I'd also like to thank all of those people that were essential to helping me pull this all together and for their belief in this book and a random guy asking them about ghosts: Dr. Tim Barth; Sam, Billy, the staff of Bruce Hall, and the University of North Texas (Ca-CAW!); the staff of the Dallas Public Library; Rick, Joy, Bridget, and The Association for the Study of Unexplained Phenomena; Shawn and the staff of The Catfish Plantation; Ernesto and the staff of the historic Menger Hotel; Judith and the staff of the USS Lexington Museum on the Bay; Ben, *The Skeptical Inquirer* magazine, and the Committee For Skeptical Inquiry; Clare and the Center For Inquiry of Austin; JJ and the Texas Paranormal Advanced Research Team; Jimmy, Chrissy, and Wide Awake Paranormal; Sandy, Andy, Lulu, and the staff of the Freestone County Historical Museum; the citizens of Fairfield, Texas; Robin and SpiritRescueOnline.com, the citizens of Grapevine, Texas; and Emily Mulkey for her amazingly atmospheric photographs.

Perhaps most importantly, thank you to all you spirits hard at work haunting across the Lone Star State — without you there wouldn't be a whole lot to write about!

Finally, thank you, the reader, for joining me on this adventure. Enjoy...and BOO!

Howdy Partner!

For many of us, the movie "Ghostbusters" captured our imaginations. I, on the other hand, remember being carried out by my parents in hysterics from The Chateau Theater in Irving, Texas, during the first few moments of the librarian scene. Growing up ghosts, monsters, and creatures of all kinds interested me like they did many kids. As a child of the 1980s, I regularly re-enacted video game moments and movie scenes in my neighborhood as soon as I set foot off of the school bus and hurried to the not-so-secret safety of my tree-house (one of three) in my backyard. There I wielded my own ectoplasm containment unit (a shoebox) and proton pack (my backpack with vacuum hose attached) and dreamed of finding and fighting dark spirits around the world.

Just like many of you I looked forward to a day when I would be lucky enough to see my own real ghost. That's not to say that I didn't think that there weren't already some around. For instance, I could swear that my grandparent's middle bedroom was absolutely haunted. Each of the grandkids stepped a bit faster past the doorway to that dark, foreboding room, certain that some unseen boogeyman would strike. In hindsight (and with a little bit more maturity than I had as a 9-year-old), I am fairly certain that there was never anything to really be afraid of.

I read *Scary Stories to Tell in the Dark* and *Ghost Rider* comics and was entranced by TV shows like "Unsolved Mysteries" and "Sightings." The older I got, the more curious I became. There were lots of photos, recordings, and eyewitness testimonies that strongly suggested to me that there had to be something more to ghosts than mere dust particles and mass hallucinations.

My curiosity died off...only to rise from the grave to recapture my interest during high school. I was too old for trick-or-treating, but I was still interested in finding answers to my questions about real haunted places and the ghosts that reached out and spooked people from time to time. The problem was that there seemed to be too many differing opinions and no solid explanations as to what was really going on with all this ghost stuff.

Some friends and I decided it would be a neat idea to take a trip to Jefferson, Texas, during my freshman year of college and stay in an old historic hotel to see if we could run into an actual ghost. I'd been to the hotel before and was skeptical that we'd see anything remotely paranormal at all.

I was wrong on that occasion.

In one single experience, I was convinced it was true. Other visitors to that hotel had seen things over the years, and local police officers were reported to have been uneasy going upstairs alone. When confronted with something unexpected and unlike anything you've ever encountered, your mind struggles to connect the dots and make sense of what just happened. When asked what it was that I had experienced, my response was shaky and fragmented. I had been hit by a ghostly train — just like Ernie Hudson!

I continued on with my life and graduated from the University of North Texas, got my first job, and met my future wife. Life was going great, and while the occasional episode of "Ghost Hunters" caught my attention, ghosts were again buried in the grave. It was either by chance or fate that I came across a book about Dallas ghosts that I bought for my brother (a confirmed ghost believer/hunter) as a gift. As a result, a random question came to my mind and struck me in a profound way: "Was I spooked by ghosts?" Maybe enough time had passed and in the decade or so that followed my own sighting I'd had enough time to process that split second or two and change my mind about ghosts. Instead of being afraid of them or at least shocked by what I felt was the reality of my own chance encounter, I wanted to face those instinctive fears and challenge my beliefs to see what I would find.

I don't think I'm alone in this personal mission. I'd argue that ghosts are more popular today than ever before. I don't feel we've moved much farther forward in our understanding of what ghosts actually are. Ghosts intrigue many of us; they challenge our beliefs. They dare us to either believe or disbelieve in them. They thrill and in some ways terrify us.

Over the next year I would set out to get to the bottom of ghosts, and I invite you to tag along with me. Like so many others striking out into the unknown I decided to start in my own backyard, Texas. I'm not a 'Ghostbuster.' I'm just a regular guy on an unfamiliar path. Like you,

I have a job, people I love, family, and friends. What I will discover, we will discover together. On our journey we'll visit old buildings, gloomy corners, and, along the way, meet some interesting people with some scary stories to tell. We'll bump into paranormal investigators, an internationally well-regarded skeptic, a university professor, business owners, a friendly psychic, and more in our search for spirits and answers. So grab a flashlight partner, wear your ten-gallon hat loose, and keep your mind open…as we strike out into the unknown and challenge our beliefs as we confront the ghosts of Texas!

Ghosts 101

As I looked out the window I could see the sun sinking slowly down to the horizon. As people walked through the lobby of the North Richland Hills public library, I cleared my throat and stared anxiously at my tape recorder. Even in this quiet library, I secretly hoped no one passing by would overhear the conversation to come. It was a few minutes before 7 p.m. and I waited with anticipation for my interview with Tim Barth. As I began searching for people to talk to about ghosts, I started at the place most people in search of the truth do: Google. A few clicks and I came across Dr. Barth, a professor of psychology at Texas Christian University. Dr. Barth had an interest in parapsychology, ghosts, and other unexplained phenomena, for which he taught the occasional class. I wanted a good jump-start on the journey I was about to begin, and I wanted to meet someone that, like me, searched for answers.

A blast of cool air intruded upon me like a phantom cold spot just as in walked Tim, the epitome of what I imagined a professor would look like: buttoned-down shirt (check), well-worn jacket (check), professor-y glasses (check), a collection of books under his arm (check). He said hello and presented a friendly handshake.

Without knowing how best to dive into the topic, I deferred to the list of questions scribbled on my notepad and decided to see where the conversation would take us. I wanted to know why ghosts and haunted places were generally brushed off as a subject fit for only friendless World of Warcraft gamers and not the average, everyday person.

"Well, to answer that, I don't quite know! I teach classes in parapsychology and at the beginning of each semester I ask the students to share their stories and experiences. One year I had a football player share an experience. He had a story about his grandmother and she lived somewhere out in the country. She was sitting in her home all alone and all of a sudden she's watching TV and all the electricity went off in the house. Then, none of the lights came on, just the television, and out of the television, she claimed, a face of something that didn't look human looked like it was scanning the room," Tim continued, recalling the student's telling of the incident.

"This is what was interesting — I said, 'What do you think about this?' The student had said before that he was a skeptic, and I asked him, 'So does this make you less skeptical?' He said, 'Well no, not really.' And so I say 'okay… does that mean that you think your grandmother is a liar or embellishes things? And he said, 'Oh no, she would never do that!'"

"Okay… so if you don't think she embellishes, do you think it definitely happened? 'Oh definitely, she wouldn't lie about something like this.' Yet, it doesn't affect your belief in these kinds of things? 'Absolutely not,' he said, and that kind of thing, to me, is very interesting because it's like there's some kind of disconnect between what we experience and what we're willing to believe. How is that modified? How can you make that connection, at least on the outside, seem more logical?" Tim asked.

"I think part of it is that there is a tendency to want to be mainstream, to be rational, and we've been taught from an early age that those things don't exist. That's crazy."

"We learn early on that it's not part of our western culture, those things don't happen. Scientists take extreme points of view. I'm a scientist and I try not to! An extreme point of view means if you can't prove it in a laboratory it doesn't exist. That includes God, life after death… If you can't prove it in a lab, it's not part of my belief system," Tim said, a bit discouraged.

"Now, I don't want to step on any toes here, but there are also a lot of people that talk about this as being evil and demonic. There's even another reason to not really study it, because if you're studying it, it's probably not something you should even be talking about," Tim said.

As I listened and sipped at my coffee, I nodded my head in silent understanding.

"I've had this happen where students in my class have come up and told me, 'everyone in my church is praying for me'," Tim said, obviously troubled by those upset students.

"I deal with that very seriously. I say, 'Well, you know, maybe you shouldn't take it then if it really disturbs you…', and they say, 'Well I'm really interested'. I can say well, to my knowledge, no one has ever died after taking my class! No one has gone off to a life of crime. No one has joined any satanic cults as far as I know. Maybe it's happened, but I don't think it has! So, you know, I think there are a lot of reasons why we don't accept it. Yet, the majority of people I would say, in surveys in America and other places have had these types of experiences."

Ghosts are always there, from birth until death, and yet no one usually wants to openly and seriously talk about the subject. Halloween in the United States is thirty-one days in a row of people celebrating ghosts and monsters. That doesn't take into account all of the other celebrations of the dead found across different cultures. People are attracted to the idea of an afterlife, and I wonder if there's something similarly taboo about ghosts and sex. From a psychological standpoint, death and sex are two things that get the heart racing and the blood pumping! Wild car chases, sexy strangers and ghosts jumping out of dark rooms titillate us as humans, these things excite us at a very basic level, I thought, explaining my hypothesis to Tim.

"Well, yes, I think you're right. I think it's that we treat it as something dead on the side of the road, 'Oh yeah, what's that?' or 'Oh, I shouldn't be looking at that!' It's some approach/avoidance kind of a thing. But science disappoints me here. Science is supposed to walk the line of being a skeptic and also being open-minded to new discovery. A good scientist isn't in the extreme in either case; they've got to walk that line: stay skeptical and critical, but yet keep their minds open to new things and to new discoveries. What's happened over time is that scientists have moved further and further into being cynics, which is the extreme of being skeptical. Extreme in the other direction is being naïve, you don't want to be naïve and you don't want to be cynical. You want to be somewhere in-between."

"It's unfortunate that there are skeptic organizations. I don't know if you've come across any of their websites, but you should do it before you go too far into this because I believe, as a scientist, that they are a real threat to good science, and this is why. They take such an extreme position, they belittle these experiences that people have had that are supposed to be the cornerstone of inquiry — you know, what we experience in the world, well that's where you start and try to understand! The arguments they use are extreme in and of themselves. Most of them aren't scientists. Look at their credentials: they're philosophers, they're magicians, they're academics, they're psychologists (which elicits a good laugh from both Tim and I), but they claim they carry the banner of science and rational thinking."

"Yet, if you look at their arguments and are willing to be critical of their criticisms, you find that they are making many of the same errors that the really naïve people are making, arguments that are just irrational with no basis in logic. 'No that doesn't exist, therefore, if it seems like it's happening we know it must be something else'…that sounds circular to me! Yet, they are perfectly fine with that because they feel the likelihood of something outside our sense of what nature is… the potential for something like that to happen is so small we shouldn't even entertain it. To me, that is moved so far from open-minded inquiry, it diffuses the beauty and importance of science. So I see those skeptics as a danger to the scientific inquiry; I believe they have the potential to turn some people off, to turn the public off…like, 'Scientists are saying that I'm crazy or whatever, or that I'm just naïve, or that I'm stupid.' Therefore, there's going to come a time, I believe, as people have more and more of these experiences, which seems to be happening by some people's counts, that science is going to be thrown away as something that's not really important," Tim said with a genuine hint of concern in his voice.

Wait! That would place the burden of proving elusive phenomena on unqualified people, leaving them alone to defend their claims and be charged with recreating something potentially very rare in an unscientific way without knowing what they're looking for! What if ghosts were a couple of different things? A rare bug? A temporary hallucination? A dead person that won't move towards some existential light?

What about the people out there that like the idea of taking a flashlight and camera and heading off into some dark building or cemetery at night? Most people are content to just watch horror movies or read Stephen King novels. What made venturing into spooky places so appealing to people?

"It allows [them] to escape the world for at least a brief period of time. I mean I have it, too. I don't think about this stuff on a regular basis — I just couldn't function if I did! On the other hand, life's interesting. Right around this time of the year, when I'm getting ready to teach the summer course, I allow my mind to start kind of thinking along these lines. It feels good, it feels interesting, and at some level it feels important," Tim said.

Tim reflected on his own personal interest in the paranormal, an interest that somehow seemed to renew something in him. It seemed to allow him to creatively wonder and to search for answers to bigger questions. It was infectious to listen to.

"It's uncharted territory, and I feel like guiding those students' thinking and opening their minds to either being more critical or to be more open to these possibilities. Whatever they seem to be not, I try to move them in the opposite direction. So at the end, they're totally confused. By the end of this course, my goal is to have you totally confused! You know, I find that like I'm challenging them, like I'm making them work their brain muscles that they don't normally work, and to not just take things for granted."

There are countless practical possibilities to explore before you even go down the road of considering something supernatural as an explanation. What if a ghost just turned out to be a rare case of the brain tricking you? What if in only even one percent of cases it's found to be something else? Maybe it was someone's consciousness surviving after their body had finally failed them, I thought. What would that revelation mean? For a spiritually inclined person it's a greater answer to a bigger mystery, something much more far-reaching to consider than just a single haunted house.

"It's proof. It's there, that's something. My consciousness and my existence don't end if tomorrow I get into a car accident and die, and I think that's comforting. We all have an anxiety towards death. I've run across many people since I've started teaching this course who have had family members that have died — you know, parents, partners or

whatever — who have said, 'If there's anyway I can come back eternally young, anyway I can come back, I will.' That's comforting not only to the person who's dying, but also to the person left behind."

"I know a person who that happened to. She claims that her husband leaves her pennies around the house, everywhere... She picks them up, and she puts them away and she's absolutely confident that she'll go back and they'll be there again. I can tell that's a great source of comfort for her," Tim said, adding that the reason for the woman believing is more important because it helped her cope with a life lived without her soulmate. It's a person that she knew — a husband — that even after the finality of "till death-do-us-part" still stopped by to let his wife know he loved her.

Of course, the real explanation could be that there was just a lot of loose change scattered about the lady's house. Is it odd? Certainly. Would it be undeniable proof of a ghost? Not very compelling proof if you're a skeptic, but what if we wanted to prove to others that ghosts do exist without falling back on the old 'well, you'd just had to have been there' line? What would it take to convince all of the naysayers? What photo or video clip would cause them to throw their hands up and shout 'Hallelujah!'? Could any one bit of evidence ever sway the masses to truly believe what so many claim to encounter is real?

"I don't think so," Tim began in answer to my question. "I really believe that no matter what you show skeptics in the hopes of making them less skeptical, they're going to come up with a way to discount it. I really believe that. I do believe that there's enough ways to fake these things, or alter what you're seeing, or maybe in more of a benign way just think you're getting something else. Orbs, for example, I've talked to a couple of leaders of ghost groups and they're pretty convinced that in most cases orbs are dust particles. The way they know that is that they've taken a dusty pillow, patted it, taken a picture and they've seen orbs."

Suddenly, I felt as though I needed to wear a surgical mask everywhere I went so as not to inhale too many spirits. What a disturbing thought!

"On the other hand, there are some photos of orbs that ghost hunters are convinced are real," Tim said, pulling out a few photos.

Most of the photos appeared to have been taken outside in a backyard or out on a dirt road, and the orbs they contained looked quite strange. These orbs had movement, an unusual color, and an unnatural brightness. Some looked like miniature constellations set against the backdrop of an un-extraordinary tree. These bright, nebulous globs, whatever they were, was something else.

It was tough to dismiss these as mere specks of dust or a crazy insect flight path. We discussed the differences in photos that a real connoisseur of orbs could make between what were most likely just light reflections in some dusty room versus self-illuminating balls of light the size of a fist clearly moving through the air, something that the photographer most-likely didn't see when the picture was taken. It was hard to say, but it was encouraging that there before me were some really intriguing photos that made me stop and ask myself the question — what if I tried to fake something like this with a regular camera? How would I possibly do this, and why? What would be the gain for me, or anyone, in faking this? Maybe if someone were trying to pull a fast one to get a few minutes of airtime on the nightly news they'd create a faked photo. People for some reason do this sort of thing all the time, they Photoshop-in a UFO over their house, or run past a game camera on a ranch in a gorilla costume hundreds of yards away to create a deceptively interesting looking Bigfoot sighting. But these photos were basically old close-ups of leaves on trees and not anything that would immediately made me think that what I was looking at was a ghost. These orbs were something that the people taking the photos didn't appear to see when the shutter flashed. Could they be proof that ghosts were somehow invisibly walking (or floating) by?

When I think of most ghost stories they always seemed to describe the appearance of a full-bodied apparition. Scary ghost stories are not the odd orbs caught on camera; they're the ones that are about the faint voice in your ear, the unfamiliar one hissing your name with perfect, whispered clarity in an unfamiliar place. Many reported encounters with ghosts are unsettling, tangible experiences for people. Are they all mistaken or pathological liars? I was curious to know what a psychology professor thought about this. Why would people clearly upset after supposedly seeing a ghost imagine such a thing?

"I wouldn't say it's 100 percent by any means, but I would say the vast majority of these people are very believable, very confident — they're not just trying to pull the wool over your eyes. I have very good friends who are very rational, though I being their friend may be a mark against them, and they've had one or two experiences that they just can't explain," Tim laughed. "These people...they're not nuts. I mean, they are just not nuts."

Some of the best-known haunted spots are widely reported because so many people have experienced the same things over and over again and consistently arrive at the conclusion that what is happening must be paranormal. Doesn't that lend even more credibility to the single incidents reported over time? Many places have ghostly activity that has been reported by hundreds of people over the span of years. Shouldn't those cases be looked at more closely due to all of the reports?

"Those are the most compelling cases — when different people who don't know each other report basically the same thing and there's documentation, especially documentation as to what each individual saw when they didn't know what to expect to see and the specific

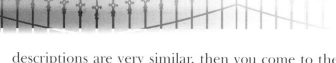

descriptions are very similar, then you come to the conclusion, in my opinion, that there really is something paranormal there, or, that there's something about the physical layout of the area that lends itself to some sort of common illusion, misperception, whatever you want to call it. Which is equally interesting in my opinion. Maybe not equal, but still interesting."

Maybe it's not that a room is actually haunted, maybe it's just creepy looking. There are dark rooms, places that just seem uncomfortable to us due to lighting, temperature, humidity... Maybe we equate those uneasy feelings to that feeling of being watched. Or maybe we just think of all the scary movies we've seen that featured a killer stalking some poor girl through a dark basement, and suddenly we realize that we're standing in similar surroundings and let our imaginations get the best of us.

"I tend to think, whenever I start hearing a lot of negative stuff, and a lot of life-threatening stuff that I tend to become more skeptical. I just don't think that's the direction these things mostly go. I think they can on occasion, but you know when it gets down to, you know, 'the ghost has murdered three people, or five people, or seven people and everyone in the house is dying left and right', that's crazy, come on," Tim said incredulously.

Thankfully, most of the so-called genuine haunted house reports recount simple occurrences. Spooky, mind you, but certainly not full-bodied apparitions of chained corpses violently stabbing the living occupants to death in the middle of the night before fading back away into the window curtains. I imagined that people involved in these types of hauntings would probably start to question reality. Their own sanity must get put through the ringer in really extreme cases. Imagine hearing voices from across the room, over your shoulder, or in the shower. The shiver you get when you know someone just walked behind you in the laundry room. Now imagine you couldn't prove any of it. You had no reason for it, didn't watch scary movies or play the latest horror video game. How would you explain that otherwise irrational fear to your family? Your friends, would they believe you? How long would these strange happenings have to go on before you had to either consider the fact that you might just be crazy, or maybe crazier still, it was all actually happening and you had no control over it? What if the ghost was a small child, one that never showed itself, but always piled keys and silverware in a nice pile on your bed once every few days? Imagine that you can hear this child laugh faintly over the sound of your TV, but never enough to know for sure if your mind was just connecting unrelated audio dots and imagining it as something else. Even then, without any perceived malicious intent, I'd be scared! And what if a ghost were more brazen, more overt in its actions? What if a spirit seemed to want to hurt or intimidate you? Most people probably wouldn't know how to cope, and even in rare instances, I would think most people would have just as hard a time coping with non-physical interactions that still disrupted their lives, causing late nights, restless sleep, and the fear of what would happen next.

"I had a student once in one of my classes. This is just another negative experience... She claimed she moved into a two-story place and her kids would sleep in an upstairs bedroom. She claimed that many times as she walked by the top of her stairs she would feel like she was shoved, as though some unseen person was trying to push her down the stairs. So there are some negative things, but I tend to think those aren't the majority."

Well, that will help me sleep better tonight, I thought! When you stop and think about a ghost, most people picture a misty form in flowing white sheets or a fleeting glimpse of something just out of sight. How could a mist attack you? Since when did invisible-to-the-naked-eye blobs of smoke pose any harm to a person at all? In short, why should we need to worry about ghosts?

"If you think about ghosts and energy, it's very consistent with the laws of physics in that energy is never destroyed. Energy persists, it may change forms or intensity, but it's still going to be some level of energy. That idea seems to make it credible the fact that what we have here is a physical body but there's something that's going to persist afterwards. I don't think anybody can deny that. The question is that whatever it is that persists, is that something that's conscious? Is that something that resembles us in some way or form, or does it just sort of dissipate into the milieu of the universe and just becomes entwined in everything else? And you know, I don't know," Tim shrugged.

I've often wondered what the human 'spirit' is. 'Am I who I am because of my skin, my bones or my vital organs? Is my heart part of my soul? If you transplanted my heart into someone else, would I go along for the ride?' I know there's probably more than a few romantic comedies/ horror films out there in which such a transplant caused the recipient to suddenly have some possessed arm only to find later the donor was a serial killer, but seriously, I've long thought that maybe our bodies were sort of the hardware and our spirit was the operating system that made an otherwise inanimate hunk of plastic, wires, and keys an interactive object able to send and receive data, save files to memory, and be switched over to another computer or have a battery replaced when the system crashed to avoid the scrap heap.

"Well there's also this idea...it's called many different things, the term I'm familiar with is 'super ESP', and that is this idea that whenever I do this," he said as his hand hit the shiny metal table surface, "I've

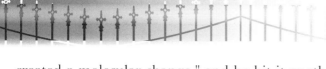

created a molecular change," and he hit it another few times. "It's not the same as it was before I did that. There's this thinking out there, and it's largely unsubstantiated other than that theoretically it could happen, that if there's some sort of traumatic event that occurs, it somehow impregnates the physical space around it. Then, and this is where it gets kind of odd, if the conditions are right, whatever that means, somehow it's released like a videotape and people experience it again and again if the conditions are right. That's why several people can have the same experiences at different times, not knowing each other — because it's being released because the conditions are right. So there are several different possibilities."

By this point my mind considered the many possibilities of what ghosts could be and what it could all mean. Sensing this, and having run the gamut of ghostly topics with essentially a complete stranger, Tim and I sat in a few Zen-like moments of silence. We leaned back into our chairs, checked the time and saw that the night sky out the windows now engulfed the library.

We gathered our things up under our arms, shook hands, and looked forward to meeting again. As we walked towards the doors we talked about a few of our favorite books on ghosts, one of which was surprisingly *Spook* by Mary Roach.

"You know, I love the last part of that where she said basically, 'Do I believe in ghosts? Why the hell not!' he said with a chuckle. "Whatever she said, I don't know what her exact words were but it was sort of like 'it made life more interesting, so I think I'm going to believe in them', and that's a valid response."

As I fumbled for my keys and took in a deep breath of fresh spring air I felt energized, excited, and fairly certain after talking with Dr. Barth that there was something to this ghost stuff after all, maybe more than I'd ever imagined. It was hard to come to any other conclusion in that moment other than that this well-informed man honestly believed ghosts existed.

Driving home, my headlights barely fought off the darkness long enough to reveal the lanes. As I teetered on the edge of consciousness on the couch while watching DVDs that night, my mind raced and then settled before finally falling asleep to the flickering glow of the TV. I awoke at 3 a.m. exactly. Frozen on my TV were the faces of the cast of "Newsradio" eerily staring at me from a static menu screen. The den was still and quiet, and it was almost as if in the dead of night, something had quietly awoken me. As I turned off the lights, climbed into bed, and flicked off the night-stand light, the click shattered the eerie silence.

I slept the rest of the night…the comforter covering my head.

They Call Her Wanda

Wanda, a young woman at the University of North Texas, is a student that some say is the permanent resident of Bruce Hall. She died, according to legend, up in the fourth floor attic of the building over fifty years ago, but then again...she may never have existed at all.

When I first began digging into the Wanda legend, I started by delving back into the university's past. Bruce Hall officially opened in 1946 and in the years that followed Wanda's presence became closely associated with the dormitory. Originally the building was intended to be an all-female residence hall and during that time female students were required to live on-campus. Despite my efforts, including reviewing author James L. Roger's exhaustively detailed book *The Story of North Texas: From Texas Normal College, 1890, to the University of North Texas System, 2001*, there weren't a lot of great leads to help me match the ghostly stories to historical facts. It was difficult to even track down exactly when the stories began, but it was certainly several decades ago if you go by the number of Facebook stories various alumni have shared in recent years.

What is the legend? It changes depending on whom you ask. It's the story of a young woman who died in Bruce Hall many years ago, most would say back before 1950, which would place it within the first few years of the dorm's opening. "Wanda," as she has ever-since been called, was distraught and alone. She was a pregnant student with nowhere to turn. Growing more desperate and with no one to confide in, she ascended the stairs to the top floor of Bruce Hall and locked herself away in the dark, empty attic. It is rumored that her unborn child was conceived with an unnamed professor or some other man holding a position of prominence within the university or greater community. After hours of gut-wrenching, heart-breaking crying, Wanda supposedly calmed herself. Tears still etched into her cheeks, her mind flirting precariously on the fraying edges of rationality, she sat down in a forgotten chair situated by one of the attic windows.

She couldn't bring a child into the world; after all, she had no means to protect or provide for it. The father denied the child was his, which drowned Wanda's hopeful thoughts of becoming a mother in unforgiving,

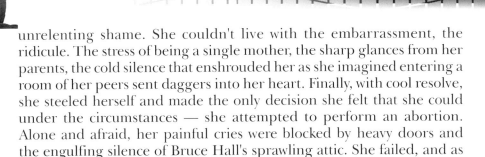

unrelenting shame. She couldn't live with the embarrassment, the ridicule. The stress of being a single mother, the sharp glances from her parents, the cold silence that enshrouded her as she imagined entering a room of her peers sent daggers into her heart. Finally, with cool resolve, she steeled herself and made the only decision she felt that she could under the circumstances — she attempted to perform an abortion. Alone and afraid, her painful cries were blocked by heavy doors and the engulfing silence of Bruce Hall's sprawling attic. She failed, and as her life slipped away behind the curtain of this world, she instead gave birth to one of UNT's most enduring legends.

I was an undergraduate at UNT when I first heard about the reports of strange occurrences in Bruce Hall. Not about the ghost, but about "the Brucelings" — the residents of Bruce Hall. They were the eclectic students, the band nerds of campus (at least from what I vaguely recall). Aside from the stories shared on campus and a few *NT Daily* articles that sporadically appeared every few years, there was little to go on. I first contacted the Housing department and an anthropology professor I'd had when I was an undergrad, neither of which had heard much more than I had. With nothing but the first name "Wanda" (which could have been a nickname for all I knew), hunting down any form of death certificate in Denton County was, I was told, about as good as my chances of literally walking up to and shaking hands with Wanda herself.

In speaking with a few different alumni and university staff, I was able to identify a few specific places to look for Wanda, which was great considering there are over 492 individual resident spaces within Bruce Hall! I had arranged to meet with a Resident Assistant named Samantha the day after every student in the building had left for the summer. Bruce Hall would be relatively empty, and the university graciously invited me to visit and wander the silent corridors to my heart's content! This would be a big undertaking — it was a large building and one that I was familiar with when I passed on my way to class years ago, but I had never really explored it before. I called in backup and asked a longtime friend of mine to tag along.

It was a sunny Sunday in May, a day that couldn't have been less frightening if the day itself had given it 'the old college try'! As I hit the intercom buzzer at the front door, Nick and I exchanged glances, excited to be on my first ghost hunt. It was hot as hell outside, late afternoon and a balmy 100 degrees. A young guy's voice answered, statically emitting a bored 'hello' from the entrance speaker.

"Hi, we're here to meet Sam," I replied.

A moment later, a young girl wearing a black baseball cap, a t-shirt, jeans, and sneakers opened the door.

"Hey, you're Nate?" Samantha asked politely.

"Yeah, that's me! This is my friend, Nick," I replied excitedly. "You're Sam, right?"

"Yeah, come on in, I'll give you the tour," she said with a shrug and a wave of her hand. As we walked in the front entryway, old copies of the *NT Daily* filled wire baskets and a very institutionalized-looking stairway greeted us on both sides. Up the first small flight of stairs was a large black-and-white cartoon mural that caught my eye. "Bruce" was spelled out beneath a painting on the wall of Bruce Hall, with tiny details hidden throughout the "haunted house" appearance of the cartoon-ified dorm, like the giant albino squirrel attacking the roof, the witch-like cafeteria worker serving 'gruel'…and there, gliding out the top left attic was the wispy form of a long-haired beauty in a white dress. Not five minutes in yet and we'd already seen Wanda, though I hoped for a much more personal encounter!

The dorm looked as I would expect it to if hundreds of kids had upped and left in the last twenty-four hours. It looked disheveled, abandoned and not unlike the quirky haunted house mural graced across the stairwell wall. Papers were strewn around the front desk, old flyers were stapled to message boards on the walls, and mops and trash cans were strewn about. The place felt very old, and when I looked at Nick we sort of smiled and shared the only mutual single thought that came to mind: 'college.'

"So, how do you want to do this?" Sam asked as she hopped over the front desk and plopped down into an old swivel chair. She had an edgy appearance, sort of a tomboy, the kind that would out-skateboard you in front of a group of friends and then celebrate her victory with the guys while you held your head in your hands in defeat.

"Well, we aren't too familiar with the building, if you can draw us a map or something that would be great. Or, if you have the time, we'd love the guided tour. I've got a few spots in particular I'd like to hit. Basically we're not sure what we're looking for so much as what might find us, but I definitely want to hit the attic and basement if it's alright with you," I said.

With that, Sam produced a large set of jangling keys, a Sharpie, and a piece of paper to draw a map of each floor. As Sam's dorm 'treasure' map took shape, I could see that there were A, B, C, and D wings across four floors — and a hell of a lot of rooms. I was really happy to have someone who knew where they were going guiding us.

Down the long first floor hallway and downstairs seating area we went. A lone piano sat in a corner; the air tasted empty, robbed of all life with the departing of last semester's students. As we neared the stairwell we approached two pool tables situated in a back corner, both with old-style stained-glass light fixtures hanging above, and one read simply 'Wanda's Pool Hall.'

"Hehe, wow, Wanda is a real celebrity here! First she had a featured spot in the mural up front and now her own pool table!" I said.

In doing some research I'd come across an alumni named Billy who used to be the head RA at Bruce Hall in the early 2000s. During our conversation, we discussed Wanda and Billy's own experiences prior to my visit.

"Well, there was one occasion where I was living in one of the wings of the dorm by myself, and I really hadn't heard much about the haunting, let alone had my own experience," Billy began.

"I'd locked the entire place up tight, and I had the only keys that could have opened the exterior doors to let someone in. I was used to making regular checks through the building, and so I knew I was alone. It was late afternoon, and I went down to the pool tables and just sunk a few shots to pass a little time. After I'd knocked a few in, I racked all of the balls and left them in the center of the table, then set the pool cue off to the side and walked down the hallway back towards my room," Billy continued.

"I wasn't more than a few steps around the corner down the hall, and I distinctly heard the pool table balls break. It stopped me right there, mid-step!" Billy laughed, and I almost heard a slight tingle up his spine sounding in his voice.

"Well, I just sort of froze for a minute, I mean, it was real. I heard it just as if someone broke at the table I was just at, and since I knew I should have been completely alone in the building I turned around and headed right back to see who was there. Nothing! I turned the corner, and no one was there, the table was just like I'd left it seconds ago. That sort of shook me! After that, I wasn't sure…" Billy said with an incredulous tone to his voice.

"Well, I could imagine!" I said. "I'd have become a quick believer! So you think it was Wanda that you heard?" I asked.

"That's the thing," Billy said, "I've heard all the stories about Wanda, but not a lot of people have ever reported a woman or anything specifically. To tell you the truth, and you may know more about it than I do, I don't know there is a lot of history tied to her. I've heard of the stories in books and other places about people having seen a woman walk around a corner, or a door slam, but aside from my experience there isn't a lot I'm personally aware of as happening due to a ghost. Although there was a guy I knew who was cleaning up downstairs one night when he said a trash can was thrown against a wall next to him, and he sounded very shaken. So, I suppose if that happened to me, I'd be scared too! I'm not sure… Could be a ghost, I'm not saying it isn't possible."

"So, do you think maybe it's something else?" I suggested.

"Well, I think there is something people have seen or heard from time-to-time, but I'm not sure I'd say there's a lot of activity. All I'm saying is think of how many students walk through a university dorm room each day, or even each year. It's not something people like to talk about or dwell on, but if I had to guess I'd imagine there are a lot more students that have died on campus over the years than just Wanda," Billy said.

That comment made me pause. Maybe the legend of Wanda is what people talked about around Halloween and on dark, stormy nights at Bruce Hall, but who's to say that some 'Bruceling' didn't conjure up some dark spirit in their dorm room using an Ouija board? Or that another student might have once overdosed or died of some other cause across the long decades? It made me think: if I was some poor wandering soul, would I be upset at people having me pegged as someone who never existed? It seemed to me that ghosts might suffer from the occasional case of mistaken identity.

With the hall almost completely unoccupied, this was a perfect chance to challenge Wanda (or whoever roamed the halls) to a friendly game of pool. I racked the balls on "Wanda's" table, and then we followed Sam around the corner for the rest of our guided tour. I wondered if maybe Wanda would take the opportunity to play a bit while we toured her sprawling home!

We decided to start from the bottom and work our way up. I'd heard a few stories attributed to Wanda or some other malicious ghosts supposedly hanging about the basement, which was a prohibited place seldom seen by most students. In the few stories I was able to uncover it was suggested that this area was once a shower facility where a young man was brutally attacked by several other men and murdered in cold-blood, leaving an angry spirit to occupy the dark belly of the building. After a little checking, this particularly gruesome story seemed a bit too sensational to be believed and nothing in the building's history turned up to support such a gory tale.

"To be honest, it does get kinda creepy in here at night," Sam said with a laugh. "At times like this when the hall is quiet, especially at night, you get this weird feeling." Her keys out, she walked around the corner to a brown, narrow door tucked away in a corner and fumbled with the lock. The door honestly looked like it was the first door invented, clearly as old as the building. A small, red sign read "Authorized Personnel Only" and, with no windows, the sign seemed more than a bit foreboding.

"And here we go…" Sam said in a spooky tone.

"What do they got in there, King Kong?" I asked in my best Jeff Goldblum impersonation.

"This is the boiler room. It's sort of dark, so stay close to me until I get the lights on. It's not the safest room to be in," Sam stated matter-of-factly.

Sam stayed close to the wall at our right, grasping into the darkness. I couldn't see anything, and the stark outline of the open door behind us beckoned that we return to the safe light of the real world. With a flicker and a flash, several large lights overhead sprang to life, and suddenly I could see the catwalk we were standing on and steps leading down further into the concrete and brick basement.

Even under bright lights the room just felt oppressive. My ears immediately hurt from the various sounds bouncing around wildly emanating from thick, nondescript pipes and old, unnamed apparatuses. The suffocating air, hot in our lungs, sucked the very life out of us with each breath. As we walked around, it became apparent this was originally some sort of furnace area in the basement, eventually repurposed and updated with modern generators. The floor was wet with standing water in places, and a lone, large cockroach quickly scrambled in front of us and off to the relative safety of a dark corner.

"Charming place," I said. My eyes scanned the back of the room, and we joked a bit about it needing a woman's touch, as ghost or no ghost, I doubted most people (living or dead) would find the room to be to their liking. With all of the noises and surrounding machines the scariest thing any ghost hunter might encounter here would be being tasked with analyzing recordings for any signs of EVPs.

Just when I thought I had seen one of the world's most creepiest doors, we made our way to arguably the most intimidating door I've ever seen that wasn't a prop in a haunted house amusement park. "Keep Door Closed" was stenciled on the old white door in gaudy yellow paint, scuffed from years of use. It was larger than most of the other doors and looked as though it was designed to lock something in versus keeping anything out.

"Sweet Jesus!" was all Nick managed to offer.

"Yeah, we can take a look in here if you want to," Sam said as she began to struggle with the large latch holding it shut.

"You know, this really is what I'd imagine a horror movie basement would look like," I said. "This is clearly not the safest place to be already, so we might as well toss in a ghost while we're at it!"

Sam somehow managed to unlock the door (the "Hellraiser" contraption that it was) and started to slowly slide it open sideways, as pulleys and old metal screeched and moaned. Nick and I were no real help, and looking back on it this probably wasn't our most chivalrous moment. We shifted to the side closest to the opening, my flashlight sweaty in my hand, a source of light ready to pierce the blackest night or bludgeon anything that should spring towards us when suddenly...

"GAH! Holy hell!" I involuntarily shouted as I jumped backwards from the door.

"Oh my God!" Nick let loose...as he, too, sprang away from the gaping opening.

The dark, inky-black room slowly revealed itself as the door yawned open. As we peered into the depths, eyes squinting through the murky shadows, suddenly we were met face-to-face with a pale, lifeless woman staring up into our eyes! A table had been positioned right inside the door, and on it sat the severed upper torso of the most unexpected mannequin I think I'll ever see in my life.

"That got me!" I admitted with a laugh, as the icy chills running through my veins drained out of me.

Sam laughed and peeked around the corner innocently as the door became fully opened. "Oh yeah, that," she said with a soft giggle. An old, dusty card table stood just inside, off to the left. On it was the strangest assortment of randomly discarded items:

1. The pale, upper torso of a female mannequin, complete with a 'Mean Green' dew rag covering her bald head, a poorly-positioned black eye-patch, black, white, and green garments, and an assortment of beads draped about her. The face had a truly sexy beard scribbled in with a black marker, and it caught the light in such a way so as to be a real shock for an unsuspecting visitor.

2. A lonely Mardi Gras mask, covered in years of dust, loosely discarded amongst old sheet music strewn across the table.

3. A bottle of Mr. Bubble shampoo, circa 1980.

4. A wooden chair with what looked like a couch pillow, a grey, plastic sword and an acrylic painting of an ominous-looking old man in black shirt, complete with disheveled beard and piercing eyes staring from the canvas directly into our souls.

5. A precariously perched Russian hat (you know, the furry hats with ear muffs-built-in) sitting atop the painting, appearing to almost float before us in mid-air.

"Huh. Now there's something you don't see every day," I said.
"I seriously nearly crapped myself!" Nick said with a relieved laugh.
We stepped in and looked into the back of the brick-lined corridor. It looked like an old storage area maybe used to store coal or whatever-the-hell was used to heat the building at one point. Sadly no ghosts or dead bodies, but the room still managed to startle us with a truly bizarre collection of inanimate objects just the same!

After a brief walk around the basement we decided not much was going to happen down here, and anything that might have happened would probably go unnoticed short of a full-body apparition walking right in front of us. We exited the way we came and headed upstairs to the fourth floor, ever-closer to the attic.

As we walked up the empty stairwell, I asked Sam where most students reported the ghostly happenings and asked her what her own thoughts about the haunting were based on what she'd experienced.

"Well, the fourth floor is the place that gives me the creeps," she said matter-of-factly. "Honestly, though, most students just talk about Wanda, not many see her. I can't say I've met anyone that has had an experience beyond just odd feelings some of them get when they are alone or when it's dark outside. I've only been here a couple of years, but haven't had much happen during that time, but ask anyone and they will know about Wanda," she said.

Nick began snapping photos with my digital camera as we walked around trying to get a feel of the floor plan. The heavy wooden doors and old, mismatched room numbers nailed to the tops of each door-frame definitely lent an eerie vibe to the place. The worn carpet was loaded with dust and Nick regularly captured images of small orbs (AKA dust particles) dancing in front of the shutter as we walked along our way.

The hallways had a musty, unidentifiable smell to them. My nose sifted through what smelled like a potpourri of decades of smoke, pizza, and assorted body odors. For a building inhabited by decades of music majors, though, it certainly could have been worse. I thought of the thousands of students that had roamed through Bruce Hall — countless doors opened, voices raised, tears shed — all in just this single building on campus. Many subscribe to the idea of what is commonly called a 'residual haunting,' the idea that a place like an old building or an object like a wall, for instance, could record energy from events that somehow were imprinted on it. In this particular theory Wanda might actually not be a ghost at all, but rather an odd physical outburst of energy replaying in the surrounding environment that can be perceived by people.

Could it be possible that the very environment wherein countless students played pool, slammed doors, opened blinds, or banged door-frames with drumsticks had somehow been noticed by our brains, or even odder still, actually caused the same old doors, blinds, and other objects in the hall to reenact the same actions time and time again? Weirder still, could still-living alum's actions be the cause of the haunting activity today due to how they interacted within the Bruce Hall environment as a student?

I decided it was a good idea to try to debunk a few of the claims reported over the years. There was an experience reported by a residence hall assistant — that person claimed to have seen the apparition of a

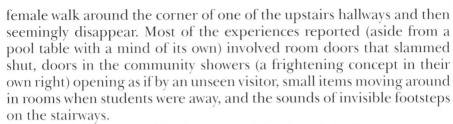

female walk around the corner of one of the upstairs hallways and then seemingly disappear. Most of the experiences reported (aside from a pool table with a mind of its own) involved room doors that slammed shut, doors in the community showers (a frightening concept in their own right) opening as if by an unseen visitor, small items moving around in rooms when students were away, and the sounds of invisible footsteps on the stairways.

Most claims seemed fairly easy to debunk and, in fact, most were. On a few of the floors Nick and I took turns opening several of the heavy wooden room doors — either all the way or partially — and each swung shut reliably due to how heavy they were. Unless the doors were propped open securely, the chances of students hearing a nearby door accidentally fall shut appeared to be pretty high and, thereby, not the telltale sign of Wanda's presence.

In a trip to one of the shower rooms, we took turns walking into the room while the other stood in a stall to see how easy it would be to see others entering. Here, too, there was a perfectly reasonable explanation. By design, the stalls were set back in a way so as to not be easily seen each time the main door to the hallway opened to ensure student privacy. As the door opened, if you looked to see who entered, the door would block your view, so it was entirely possible that students might open the door and realize that they'd forgotten their shower flip-flops and walked away leaving a scrubbing shower-dweller to call out, hear no reply, and see the door slowly close.

The claims of items moving around sounded a bit like that pesky 'lost keys' phenomena we've all experienced where the explanation has more to do with observer absentmindedness than the supernatural. After several practical tests over ninety percent of the reported claims could be explained by common causes, leaving us with no evidence to suggest anything paranormal was afoot. Our practical tests yielded conclusions that seemed to match with what Sam had told us — that there certainly may be spooky feelings from time-to-time, but little else.

Finally, we decided to unlock one of the two entrances to the attic on the fourth floor. As the legend goes, if there were to be a single area most likely to be occupied by Wanda, the lonely, seldom-entered attic in which she reportedly passed away would be the best place to look.

"I've looked in here before — it's really dark and you can't easily walk around in there," Sam said cautiously, rounding the corner ahead of us as we came to a dark corner of the fourth floor hallway.

Once unlocked, the attic door required the three of us to pull it forcibly open, as if it was clinging to some tightly guarded secrets not meant for prying eyes. After all our pulling the door stood open only a few feet, and was unwilling to open any further.

"Wow, it's pitch-black in here," I said, my eyes trying to lock onto anything in the darkness.

"Yeah, there's a back attic window on the other end that lets in a little light during the day, but even that doesn't help much," Sam replied.

"Is there any way to walk in?" Nick asked, leaning his head around the corner for a better look.

"Not really. There's a small catwalk, but it's not all that safe. You could accidentally step off of it and end up falling through the ceiling!" Sam said cautiously.

"Well, I'd rather not become the new ghost of Bruce Hall on this trip!" I said.

I clicked my flashlight on and shined it into the murky depths of the room. The attic was a ghostly moonscape of floor-to-rafter cables, swarms of old wiring, and tons of flaky, white insulation piled around the floor. A narrow walkway snaked around the corners and across the center of the area, four small wooden beams that led to the other side, and the sole source of light at a rooftop window opposite us.

"Well, if Wanda's in here, I think she has the place to herself. I don't think most people would want to be up here... It's not a very hospitable place to be," I said. "I could see how if you had access to this you wouldn't have to worry about visitors."

"Well, the odd part would be getting in, right? I mean, if you were to get in here, you'd need a key, you'd have to work against the door, walk to the other side, and be up here long enough that people would think to search for you, right? Just seems to me like that wouldn't be very plausible for a young woman to do if she wanted to secretly come up here and perform an abortion," Nick said, his mind considering several different possible scenarios.

"Yeah, of all the places to go, and that's not to say I think the attic was a much nicer place over fifty years ago than it is right now, I think a distressed woman could find a room with a bed and not a chair by an attic window if that's what she was intent on doing," I replied.

"Well, wasn't the story that she came up here during an off-season when the hall was empty? That might make sense that she could get up here unnoticed and have the area all to herself," Sam said.

"Yeah, still, wouldn't there be a place with a little more space? A chair? Anything that might look like an area resembling that in the stories?" I asked.

"Surely there's like a light up here for maintenance workers, right?" Nick asked, taking the flashlight from my hand and running it along the walls. After a moment, he called out, "Hey, what's this? That's a switch!", and reached for the wall.

As he flicked the switch up, a dim few light bulbs sprinkled sparingly throughout the attic fluttered to life, illuminating the attic. Our eyes squinted and began to make out the contents of the room better. As my gaze shifted down to turn off my flashlight, my attention quickly became fixated on something down and to my right.

There, legs buried deep and covered in years' worth of dust and insulation sat a lonely metal chair with a torn, padded seat and backrest. The chair sat at the end of the catwalk, bordered by large pipes running along the floor, clumps of the flaky insulation clinging to it like cobwebs.

"Wow. Okay... I wasn't really expecting to find a chair up here," I said, a bit surprised.

"Huh... Yeah, that is a creepy-looking chair, alright," Nick said, asking Sam, "Did you know this was up here?"

"No, I've been up here before, but didn't look around a lot or anything. I had heard about it, but it's right under your nose when you walk in here!" Sam said, apparently surprised herself.

"Well, it's certainly not too gory-looking. To be honest, even though it looks very foreboding, I can't believe if someone found a dead woman up here years and years ago, that they'd sort of say, 'Hey, leave that chair, the attic needs a chair', can you?"

"I would hope not!" Nick replied, amusedly.

"Well, Wanda, if this is your chair, it's a sad one," I said aloud. "If you are here, we're just trying to let you know we're here to listen to you if you would like to talk. I've got a little recorder here with me, and we're going to leave it outside this door for you. If you want to talk, please do so we know you're here."

With that we stepped back outside the attic, locked the heavy door again and set my recorder in the hallway next to the door and followed Sam back down to the pool table to see if anything had changed. Four flights down and the racked pool table balls had not moved a bit. We toured a few more areas with Sam downstairs and even listened to a ghostly experience she'd had when she was a young girl growing-up.

"Oh, I definitely believe in ghosts... I really think there's something to it," Sam said. "I like it here, and even though it's a little spooky here and there at times, nothing bad has ever happened to scare me or anything."

"The annual haunted house we have here every year for charity is actually scarier!" Sam added enthusiastically.

"I think Wanda is a good thing, she's sort of a good luck charm for Bruce Hall. Sort of our unofficial mascot, you know? Even if you don't believe in ghosts, you have heard of Wanda and that makes you part of the Bruce family," Sam said.

While most ghost stories tend to send people running away from haunted houses, in the case of the potentially haunted Bruce Hall Wanda did just the opposite. Sam made a good point. Whether Wanda's story was true or not didn't really matter; if you'd heard of her you were in on the secret and part of the Bruce family. Her story, what she stood for, what she stands for, isn't her supposed gruesome death — she is the spirit of the dormitory and an important tradition. Would Bruce Hall still be one of, if not the only, dorms on campus to produce an annual haunted house attraction if Wanda was in another dorm down the street? I somehow doubted that. Her eerie spirit was a perfect match for Bruce Hall's unique vibes.

Another hike up to the fourth floor and there my little recorder sat. The tiny, red recording light defiantly sat amidst the dark shadows of the corner. I switched it off and looked at the attic door. I was struck by how quiet it could be in the hall by myself, and I wondered, was anyone on the other side of the door?

As Nick and I walked out the front door with Sam, we thanked her for the extended tour and headed towards my car that sat steaming in the hot Texas sun. On the drive home, Nick reviewed the photos we'd taken while walking down the long halls.

"Hey! That's a total orb!" Nick said proudly. Of all the photos littered with small particles of dust, this one did seem to be a bit brighter and moving slightly in front of one of the many doorways.

"Yeah, but I wouldn't submit it to Ghost Hunters just yet!" I said, playing devil's advocate in this case.

That night I listened to the recorder audio of Sam, Nick, and I shuffling down the hallway, talking as we walked further away until there was nothing left but a loud, hissing silence. My ears strained to hear the faintest sound or whisper. After a few minutes, only silence seemed to engulf the brave little recorder by the attic.

What did the silence mean? Was Wanda there? Was she staring at my recorder? Did she have anything to say? Could she speak if she wanted to? Was the ghost of Bruce Hall even a 'she'? For that matter, was 'she' even named Wanda?

I wondered as the sound of electronic silence marched on, unbroken. As I heard my footsteps finally return over an hour later to retrieve and turn off the recorder, I was a little disappointed. No evidence of a ghost this time. However, was the absence of evidence, proof of absence? It

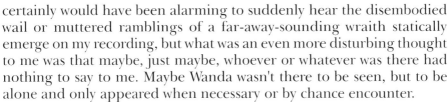

certainly would have been alarming to suddenly hear the disembodied wail or muttered ramblings of a far-away-sounding wraith statically emerge on my recording, but what was an even more disturbing thought to me was that maybe, just maybe, whoever or whatever was there had nothing to say to me. Maybe Wanda wasn't there to be seen, but to be alone and only appeared when necessary or by chance encounter.

As I turned off the recorder, I thought about that moment alone in the hall outside the attic, that brief moment that I stood and stared forward as though staring through the closed door, and wondered if someone might have been staring back on the opposite side, neither of us willing to break the silence.

The One That Got Away

Growing up around Dallas in the 1980s I had heard stories about the locally famous "Lady of White Rock Lake." In thinking back on what I actually knew about the tale, it struck me as odd that I'd never heard much about it other than the basics: a woman dressed in white walked around White Rock Lake, got picked up by passing cars, and then promptly disappeared. In hindsight, it sounded more than just a little bit scandalous.

Urban legends about 'vanishing hitchhikers' go way back. For hundreds of years people all over the world have passed down stories involving encounters with ghostly travelers. In his exceptional book *Lore of the Ghost*, Brian Haughton, an archaeologist and researcher, notes that tales of vanishing hitchhikers are "widespread throughout the world, and though most published examples come from the United States and the United Kingdom, there are also cases from Sweden, Romania, East Africa, and various other countries." Never to be outdone, Dallas residents have reported a haunting young beauty roaming the shores of their very own White Rock Lake for decades.

I think what makes these stories so compelling is that they describe chance meetings with a ghost that initially appears to be just like you or me. One could expect to come across a ghost in an old, dilapidated castle, but it is almost more unsettling to think that a ghost could appear so tangible, so real that a person could mistakenly interact with it as though they were a living, breathing human being. The vanishing hitchhiker is widely regarded as only an urban legend, which could certainly explain why these stories seem to still speak to something that is a deeply-rooted part of the human condition.

While these stories have been told for generations, the U.S. only really began to associate the term 'vanishing hitchhiker' with the phenomena following the release of Jan Harold Brunvand's book *The Vanishing Hitchhiker*. Essentially, the classic modern version of the legend begins with a person driving alone at night. The driver catches a wandering hitchhiker in their headlights and stops to give the stranger a ride. Often the passenger appears to be out-of-sorts and sometimes asks to be taken to a specific location (usually a residence) or other place where the phantom had passed away due to some sort of accident yet unknown to the driver. On the way to the destination the passenger suddenly vanishes, leaving a bewildered driver to wonder what has happened, and sometimes only a telltale item in the car is left as proof the encounter ever happened. In some variations, the driver continues on to the address given them by the paranormal passenger only to find a grim person answering the door who tells them that the hitchhiker was actually a deceased family member constantly attempting to make their way home.

When I began sifting through ghost stories around Texas, I found that while this story in particular appeared to be widely known, it didn't seem to have a lot of ectoplasm to it. In searching for the full story the facts were scarce but the legend itself seemed to have persisted in North Texas. There were more than a few variations that were purportedly the 'true' version. In researching the history of the sightings at no point was an identity proposed, let alone confirmed, as to who this phantom little lady might be.

I thought surely there was a timeline someone would have produced that could help narrow down potential candidates for the mysterious lady of the lake, or at the very least, an article that tracked the legend from the first hair-raising story to present day. All I found were bits and pieces of information citing a few dates and sightings coupled with some interesting eyewitness testimonies. As with many ghost stories, what I would find when digging up the past was almost as interesting as the terrifying tales themselves!

I knew that I was looking for a young woman who may have drowned in the lake, possibly wearing a white dress, and that any deaths connected to the lake would need to pre-date the first appearances of the reported spectral woman. When I went back to look at archived newspaper articles I was immediately staggered by the number of people that were documented as having drowned at White Rock Lake since its opening. Many deaths were those of young children and there were more than a few unfortunate souls that apparently committed suicide at various spots around the lake, or else met an untimely end due to an accident. Only a woman that drowned prior to the emergence of the first stories, though, and fitting the general description of a young lady would be a strong potential suspect for post-life patrolling of the lake.

I searched high and low, sorting through years of newspaper archives, book excerpts, and anything else I could get my hands on, as well as searching various websites. What follows was the best information I found to outline the legend of what is arguably Big D's most famous ghost.

1911: A dam and pump house at the lake are completed.

1914: Due to drought, the lake had remained empty until then. This is a key moment in time to remember as only a drowning reported following this date should be attributed to the sighting of a female specter clad in soaking-wet clothes following what she claimed was an accident on or near the lake.

May 1927: *The Dallas Morning News* reported this drowning:

> Miss Hallie Gaston, 19, a schoolteacher who resided at 238 Melba Street (in the Oak Cliff section of Dallas), drowned at approximately 9 p.m. She had been enjoying an evening aboard a motorboat with four other people traveling in roughly 20 feet of water, when suddenly, the boat sank some 200 yards from shore in an area known as "Big Thicket" near John Alexander's boat wharf. The terrible accident occurred during what was supposed to be a pleasant evening boat ride. All passengers were guests of the Worthingtons, who had held a dinner earlier that same evening at their nearby residence.
>
> The others on the boat were Miss Fama Gaston (Miss Gaston's sister) both of which were cousins of Mr. & Mrs. G .E. Worthington of 4802-1/2 Gaston Avenue, who hosted the evening, and Schuyler R. Worthington. At the time, Mr. Worthington said he could not tell what caused the boat to sink, but said that the "water just came in over the back end of it and it went under."
>
> "When I came to the top of the water I grabbed the two women and towed them to the prow of our boat," Mr. Worthington explained. Hearing the party's cries for help, nearby rescuers J. E. Sherrard, W. T. Bolling, and E. H. Cannon, Jr. "came to their aid in boats." Unfortunately the women could not swim and after Mr. Worthington had reached the boat he was exhausted, no doubt startled by the sudden turn of unfortunate events. "The brothers said they never saw Miss Hallie Gaston after the boat went under."
>
> The group searched for her for some time before finally recovering her lifeless body at approximately 12:20 a.m.

"Miss Gaston was educated in the high school at Cooper, Delta County, and at the East Texas State Teachers' College at Commerce. She recently returned to Dallas from teaching school near Palacios, Matagorda County."

She was survived by her parents, three sisters, and three brothers.

During the 1930s-40s over half a million people visited the lake each summer and it was during this time that the ghostly tales of a mysterious woman roaming the area began to emerge. In Steven R. Butler's *From Water Supply to Urban Oasis*, he cites in a section titled 'A Ghost Story' that the rumors of a lady ghost haunting the lake began to surface. The "students at Woodrow Wilson High School in East Dallas were telling the tale to one another at least as early as the 1930s, although whether it originated with them or not is uncertain," according to Butler.

Miss Hallie Gaston lived in North Oak Cliff prior to her untimely death in 1927, and Woodrow Wilson High School officially opened in 1929, two years following the tragic drowning of Miss Gaston.

However, as I would come to find, there was at least one more similarly tragic event involving a young lady that would occur not long after Miss Gaston's death.

August 1931: Miss Marian Louise Craig, 17, of "Whiteright" and Lawrence D. Newton, 24, an employee of US Airways, drowned on a Monday night around 8 p.m. Marian was visiting her brother during her stay in Dallas. Her body was located around 11 p.m, Lawrence was also eventually recovered a few agonizing hours later at approximately 2 a.m. At the time, Marian's watch was reported to have stopped at about 8 p.m., which is when it was presumed their accident occurred. Lawrence was survived by a wife and young daughter. The two were on the lake in a small, flat-bottomed, steel rowboat with no light, which made the craft difficult to see, potentially, as the sun was setting. There were reports from lake visitors that they were struck by a motorboat, but this was not confirmed. Their rowboat was eventually found at the bottom of the lake. Both victims were brought ashore and during the course of their autopsies it was ruled that the accident may have been the result of a drowning due to the rowboat sinking, as neither body displayed any signs of trauma such as cuts or other signs of violence that would suggest that their deaths had been caused in part by a collision on the lake.

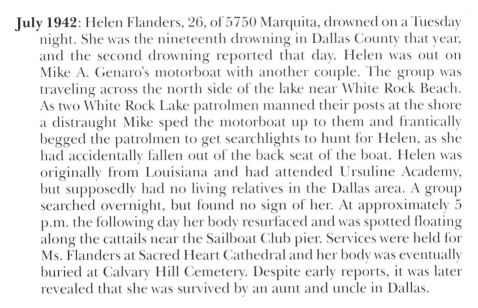

July 1942: Helen Flanders, 26, of 5750 Marquita, drowned on a Tuesday night. She was the nineteenth drowning in Dallas County that year, and the second drowning reported that day. Helen was out on Mike A. Genaro's motorboat with another couple. The group was traveling across the north side of the lake near White Rock Beach. As two White Rock Lake patrolmen manned their posts at the shore a distraught Mike sped the motorboat up to them and frantically begged the patrolmen to get searchlights to hunt for Helen, as she had accidentally fallen out of the back seat of the boat. Helen was originally from Louisiana and had attended Ursuline Academy, but supposedly had no living relatives in the Dallas area. A group searched overnight, but found no sign of her. At approximately 5 p.m. the following day her body resurfaced and was spotted floating along the cattails near the Sailboat Club pier. Services were held for Ms. Flanders at Sacred Heart Cathedral and her body was eventually buried at Calvary Hill Cemetery. Despite early reports, it was later revealed that she was survived by an aunt and uncle in Dallas.

It's interesting to note that during this time, 1942-43, one of if not the first serious study into the 'vanishing hitchhiker' urban legends had been undertaken by two American folklorists, Richard Beardsley and Rosalie Hankey. The two began collecting and studying the traditional tales from around the United States and ultimately procured seventy-nine written accounts from various places throughout the country where encounters with these phantom hitchhikers had been reported.

Of these tales, the folklorists determined that there were essentially four distinct versions of the urban legend. Over sixty percent of those gathered from sixteen states held similar characteristics, whereby a hitchhiker gave an address to the driver and upon reaching the destination the driver realized that their passenger had actually been a ghost. The folklorists considered this "Version A" of the story to be the most basic, common telling of the tale. In most cases the hitchhiker was a female ghost who had been picked up by a male driver. In fact, of the seventy-nine stories collected, forty-seven of them contained female apparitions. I mention this here because it is also around this time that there clearly was a scholarly effort made to dive deeper into these common legends, and it is around this same time that Dallas' own ghost would begin to garner her own press!

In 1943, Anne Clark wrote "The Ghost of White Rock," which was included in the Texas Folklore Society's publication *Backwoods to Border*. In it, Clark shared this story:

> A young couple parked at the lake on a hot July evening. As they turned the headlights on, the figure of a young girl in white was illuminated before them and she quickly approached the driver's side window. As the stranger drew near, the couple could see that she wore a sheer white dress and was dripping wet. In a wavering voice she apologized for the intrusion, but said that she desperately needed to get home quickly as she had been in an accident involving an overturned boat. The couple obliged her, and she climbed into the rumble seat of the car and gave them an Oak Cliff address located across town.

Could this have been Miss Gaston attempting to return home to her North Oak Cliff address?

> The couple exchanged uneasy glances — they were perplexed and a bit uncomfortable around the damsel in distress. As they approached Oak Cliff, they turned to ask the shaken passenger for more detailed directions and were shocked to find that she had vanished! Though empty, the seat was still wet.
>
> After a quick look around the car, they saw no sign of the young hitchhiker. Spooked but unable to dismiss their growing curiosity, the shaken couple continued on to the address given to them by their vanishing passenger. After they knocked on the door, a man answered, lines of worry etched deep into his face. They related to him their bizarre experience and asked the troubled-looking man if he could provide an explanation.
>
> "This is a very strange thing..." the man said, obviously affected by the bewildered couple's experience. "You are the third couple who has come to me with this story. Three weeks ago, while sailing on White Rock Lake, my daughter was drowned."

In this version of the story — and what is reportedly the first place the legend appeared — the daughter drowned while sailing, yet puzzlingly none of the recorded incidents involving a young woman drowning at the lake in the past twenty or thirty years had been in a sailboat at the time of the accident.

In 1953, well-known writer and author of TDMN's "Tolbert's Texas" column, Frank Tolbert, wrote the book *Neiman-Marcus, Texas: The Story of the Proud Dallas Store*. In it, Tolbert recounted the story of Dallas residents Mr. and Mrs. Guy Malloy who were at the time well-known display decorators at Neiman-Marcus, what was and still is one of, if not the most, prestigious stores in Dallas and maybe even the country. If you're able to find a copy of Mr. Tolbert's book, you'll find what is, I feel, the classic telling of the Dallas legend.

Sometime in the early 1940s, the Malloys were driving home late one night from a long day's work. As they drove by White Rock Lake they saw what they described as "a beautiful blonde girl" walking up from the beach. The young woman appeared to the couple's eyes to be just as solid as you or I.

"Stop, Guy. That girl seems in trouble. She must have fallen in the lake. Her dress is wet. Yet you can tell that it is a very fine dress. She certainly got it at the Store," Mrs. Malloy said to her husband. ("The Store" was a reference to Neiman-Marcus, and if anyone could spot a dress from the trend-setting store at the time it would have most assuredly been two employees familiar with the store's illustrious clothing such as the Malloys.)

The young woman actually spoke as they drew near her, and they said her voice sounded as a "friendly, cultured contralto to the couple after the car had stopped." Clearly the couple was concerned, feeling the girl was in need of assistance and was obviously involved in some form of accident at the lake. As the girl spoke to them, she asked for a ride to an "address on Gaston Avenue in the nearby Lakewood section" claiming it was an emergency. The couple was "too polite to ask" what had happened and that her long, blonde hair was drying in the night breeze as they let her climb into the car.

As the passenger-side door was opened for her, the girl "was very gracious as she slipped by Mrs. Malloy and got in the back seat of the two-door sedan." As Mrs. Malloy returned to her seat and Guy started the car, "Mrs. Malloy turned to converse with the passenger in the Neiman-Marcus gown" — only to find "a damp spot" where the girl should have been seated.

At this point, tired from a long day at work or not, it's my opinion that even salt-of-the-Earth people would be taken aback by such a creepy encounter and head for the hills! Yet, the Malloys continued on to the Gaston Avenue address the vanishing damsel gave to them, only to be met at the door by a middle-aged man. After they shared their startling experience, the man shared a now familiar story of his own. He told the couple that he had a young daughter, but that "she had been drowned about two years before when she fell off a pier at White Rock Lake."

Tolbert made a special point to note, "Mr. and Mrs. Guy Malloy, a hard-working, sober, no-nonsense couple, say very firmly that they saw a ghost."

Local author, lecturer, and all-around expert on all things Dallas, Rose-Mary Rumbley, whom I had contacted in response to a story she included in her book *Dallas Too*, also seemed to indicate that what happened to the Malloys was accurate...at least to some degree.

According to Mrs. Rumbley, her friend Barbara Rookstool told her that Barbara's father Guy Malloy had actually started the modern legend of the 'Lady of the Lake.' Rookstool stated that her father had been driving home after 2 a.m. one Saturday morning and saw the ghost by the lake. According to the conversation I had with the amazingly gracious Mrs. Rumbley, the story and subsequent legend grew out of that momentary chance sighting. Mrs. Rumbley told me she had heard that the event actually took place in the 1930s, though she couldn't recall the exact date.

There were also at least two notable reported suicides in the 1930s and 1940s. Mrs. Earl H. Davis, 38, drowned in a shallow water pit by the old Commerce Street viaduct in July 1935 while Miss Rose Stone, 35, drowned in November 1942. I mention both of these only because, while tragic, both women were in their mid-thirties at the time of their deaths and both would have died right at or following the first reported sightings and/or emergence of tales surrounding a young woman's ghost haunting the lake. Neither seemed to fit the general description of a young blonde woman, and only Mrs. Davis' passing would even be close to the same general time period that the first sightings started to be reported.

To be sure, death by suicide is a terrible thing, but is it really any more or less tragic than an accidental drowning while enjoying an evening boat ride? Many deaths have occurred at the lake over the years and each could very well warrant the possibility of a haunting as a result, but for the purposes of the legend of the lady of the lake I was looking for instances involving a young woman drowned in either the late 1920s or early 1930s.

In 1956, Tolbert wrote an article mentioning an unnamed Dallas couple (presumably Mr. and Mrs. Malloy) who were reported to have picked up the ghostly lady of the lake one night only to have driven her to a Gaston Avenue address to find that she'd disappeared from the vehicle once they had arrived. What struck me here is that Tolbert alluded to his own story contained in his book only a few years prior. In that version, the couple didn't even have the car engine started before the young spook had vanished. It was a small, but curious variance to a tale originally reported by Tolbert himself.

In 1958, Tolbert once again included a brief reference to the lady of the lake in an article and claimed that no one in Dallas had come forward reporting a sighting of the mysterious wraith in over a decade!

In 1964, Tolbert reported in an article for TDMN that an 11-year-old fifth grade girl from Cooper, Texas, named Merry Williams, wrote to him inquiring about the famous lady of the lake, wondering when interested visitors to the lake would have the best chance of meeting her face-to-ghost. Tolbert replied that he had continued to receive letters from readers asking about the famous spook and that of those, most of the reports seemed to happen in early spring more than any other time throughout the year.

Dallas resident Dale Berry wrote to Frank Tolbert in April 1964 about an experience he claimed to be "true and above reproach" that took place while he and his family lived in the 8200 block of San Fernando Way near the corner of White Rock Drive, mere minutes from the lake. Berry's letter detailed a disturbing experience he and his family had just a couple of years prior in 1962. At the time the family lived in a large two-story colonial house, which he'd initially hesitated to purchase due in part, he said, to the local legends he'd heard about the Lady of White Rock Lake.

"The first night in our new house the doorbell rang," he explained. Berry checked the front door and saw no one was there. Shortly thereafter, the bell rang a second time and again Berry checked the front door, but found nobody to be there. Berry returned to a few chores and tried to forget the odd occurrences. It was when the door rang a third time that his daughter answered the door, curious as to whom the mysterious ding-dong-ditching culprit might be. As she stepped out onto the front porch, she looked around the front yard and found no one to be haunting the lawn. Only the cool, quiet night air greeted her. As she looked down at the ground she suddenly screamed and ran into the house, slamming the door shut behind her as fast as she could. When she'd looked down, Berry described what his horrified daughter had seen. "There were puddles of water as if someone had stood there dripping, which trailed up the steps and ended in a big puddle right in front of the door," he said.

Tolbert went on to mention a woman who had written to him about a friend of hers who had drowned at White Rock Lake while at a party (possibly party boat) around 1940. At the time she said that this anonymous woman had been fashionably dressed, which echoed the reported Malloy sighting's detail of encountering a dripping-wet woman wearing a dress from "The Store." Could this have been a friend recalling the tragic loss of Helen Flanders, who drowned in 1942? It seemed like more than a simple coincidence to me upon coming across the article.

Tolbert actually wrote about the legendary ghost a few times in the spring of 1964. His regular column "Tolbert's Texas" stated that hundreds of Dallasites had called in or written to him about the "Girl Ghost of White Rock Lake." Many of the tales that were shared described very similar sightings of a young woman walking along the perimeter of the lake at night in a dripping-wet evening dress, usually in the spring.

One woman, Mrs. Lily V. Leonard, contacted Tolbert and reported that her son Bill Leonard and his wife had picked up the elusive ghost on one fateful occasion and drove her to a nearby Gaston Avenue address. "They'll swear on a stack of Bibles that this happened," she said.

This report again seemed to align with the Malloy account, and it piqued my interest because it was yet a second person that stated the wandering ghost had asked to be taken to Gaston Avenue or somewhere in that general vicinity. However, since Mr. Tolbert himself shared this story and he had already changed at least a small detail or two in the famous Malloy sighting, I was cautious to believe that this story was also not "peppered" with an additional fact or two!

It sounds as though quite a few people had seen the ghost since she was first reported a few decades earlier, yet even at that point in my research, though the story was well-known, specific details about the woman and locations involved seemed just a little too vague. No one reported a specific, verifiable encounter that had described the woman in any real detail other than to say that she was a soaking-wet blonde wearing a fashionable dress. There was no description of how old she may have been other than to suggest that she was 'young', no recollections were shared on what her voice sounded like aside from being faltering or shaky, and in the case of the Malloy encounter, quite cultured. Nothing else in particular stood out in any story and that felt odd to me as I would hope if I'd seen a ghost it would be a much more memorable moment! If you'd had a similarly shocking, confounding experience you might have a more vividly detailed picture etched into your brain leaving you desperately grasping for a rational explanation for a disappearing woman.

It is only during the 1960s that I finally came across some small additional tidbits reported about the sightings of the siren of the lake. Tolbert shared with his readers that many of the inquires he had over the years came from "mostly girl types," and that from what he'd heard the ghost usually was more prone to appear around the shores of the lake at the midnight hour.

In 1966, Ernest W. Baughman's *Type and Motif: Index of the Folk Tales of England and North America* was released. Baughman's work outlined the basic vanishing hitchhiker tale that was startlingly close to the legend of the lady of the lake:

> "Ghost of young woman asks for ride in automobile, disappears from closed car without the driver's knowledge, after giving him an address to which she wishes to be taken. The driver asks person at the address about the rider, finds she has been dead for some time. (Often the driver finds that the ghost has made similar attempts to return, usually on the anniversary of death in automobile accident. Often, too, the ghost leaves some item such as a scarf or traveling bag in the car.)"

Baughman even included a detailed classification system to identify variations on the urban legend, including the subcategory "E332.3.3.1 (b) for vanishing hitchhikers that leave items in the vehicles, unless the item is a pool of water in which case it is E332.3.3.1 (c)."

In October 1967, TDMN reported that "several hundred" teens mounted a massive nighttime search at the lake for the "'mythical' lady of the lake ghost." Initial reports were that squads of Dallas police were called to block access roads to the lake in an attempt to keep carloads of teens from hunting for the ghost in response to a local radio station broadcast in which the announcer signaled he would lead listeners to the ghost.

Police estimated that there ended up being approximately 200–250 cars that descended on the lake that night in search of the ghost, which resulted in about 1,000 people in their late teens/early twenties storming the general area. At least two-dozen riot police gathered at the lake to break up the large but generally peaceful crowd. The squad barricaded nearby Cox Cemetery (which while it may have been reported as a final resting place for the despondent spook, it doesn't not jive with any potential deceased persons that may have been connected to the reported deaths at the lake) and West Lawther Drive. The crowd was finally dispersed around 2:30 a.m., but only after helmeted police officers rushed the park as the crowd slung coins and heckling remarks to the overwhelmed police. In spite of all the commotion only two were arrested for throwing a few small firecrackers. The crowd was noisy, but ultimately not violent. By the end of the ruckus, forty-seven Dallas police officers had barricaded two major entrances to the park.

It wasn't all bad news surrounding the ghost. Around the same time a sailing club, Snipe Fleet No. 1 at the White Rock Boat Club, publicly honored the lingering shade with a race. At that time the fleet had been the nation's oldest and was part of the world's largest group of class boats. A TDMN contributor, Henry Stowers, wrote at the time, "Many people don't believe in such things, but sailors are traditionally not among such cynics."

In March 1976, despite a slow decade following the years most a-buzz with the legend surrounding the Lady of White Rock Lake, TDMN again turned a bit of attention to the ghostly tale. Laura Allen wrote this haunting statement about the upcoming spring season that year:

> "When Mother Nature turns the landscape green and dots it with spring blossoms, another lady familiar to most Dallas residents usually comes out of hiding."

Allen also seemed to take notice that the ghost had not been heard from in about a decade. She went on to cite Tolbert's then well-known version of the legend and theorized that the lost soul may have even been a suicide or a disappointed lover who had lost her life among the gentle waves; however, there were other possible explanations put forward by Dallas residents over the years, including John H. Williams Sr.'s. An operator of a lake speedboat concession, Williams reported that his son had been one of the responders to the drowning death of a girl in approximately 1956, which would have taken place several years after the legend began taking root in the area.

Also mentioned in Allen's article was the famous Malloy version of the tale, and it was here that another slightly different version of the story was included, sharing what supposedly happened once the hitchhiking ghost had arrived at her final destination. Allen added that the girl was taken to a house off Gaston Avenue by the Malloys, and that once she had disappeared the couple called upon the house and were greeted by a man at the front door who said solemnly that the poor ghost was his granddaughter who had drowned several years earlier. From Tolbert to Allen the story took yet another turn and the account of the girl ghost and her relationship to the solemn man on Gaston Avenue had changed once again!

Allen even consulted a psychic, Carl Logan, who claimed that the ghost was an "earthbound spirit" and that "nobody's ever told her she's dead and she should go away."

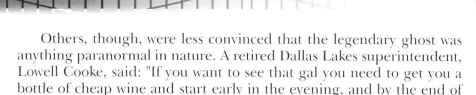

Others, though, were less convinced that the legendary ghost was anything paranormal in nature. A retired Dallas Lakes superintendent, Lowell Cooke, said: "If you want to see that gal you need to get you a bottle of cheap wine and start early in the evening, and by the end of the evening you'll see her."

A more whimsical perspective came from Jerry Wimpee, the then-current Dallas Lakes superintendent. He proposed that the legend was "something to hold onto" in a changing world.

In October 1987, Lorraine Iannello of the *Dallas Times Herald* shared an appropriately frightening Halloween update to the mostly benign historical sightings of the spook, which were reported by Phyllis Thompson and her daughter Sue Ann Ashman of Mesquite, Texas. Both claimed to have been visiting the lake one evening in 1985. While enjoying the scenery on a small boat dock on the lake near Garland Avenue, something strange floated towards them in the dark waters. The putrid object lurked just below the surface, and as it drew near it suddenly turned over to reveal its full form — that of the horrible, rotting body of a woman that let out a blood-curdling scream! As immediately as it appeared, the terrifying corpse vanished. While sensational to read, and probably more exciting to hear, this account had me laughing more than shivering at the thought.

And that, as they say, "is that." The trail, for the most part, went cold after the late 1980s. Perhaps not unlike the relatively quiet 1970s, the Lady of White Rock Lake legend seemed to have again taken a vacation from lurking along the roads circling the lake in the last couple of decades. After finally pulling together a good timeline to look back on, I began to form my own opinion of the legend and what it could all mean. There have been more than enough tragic events at the lake, many of which aren't even cited here, that suggested to me that White Rock Lake has a well-deserved reputation for being a location associated with tragedy. When attempting to narrow-down just a single candidate that fit the general description of a young woman known to have drowned early in the lake's history, there were only a few different and very unfortunate events that seemed to possibly fit the bill.

Based on the history only touched upon here, I was actually a little surprised there might not be more sightings of wandering ghosts in the area! On the one hand, there were apparently numerous reported accounts made by seemingly reliable witnesses and many more that seemed to have been reported down the long years by people who happened to have caught a glimpse of the lady of the lake. Had the stories reliably been reported every Halloween like clockwork I might have been a bit more skeptical, more willing to believe that in this case there was nothing to it all aside from a spooky tall tale to tell.

However, if we are to again entertain the notion that a haunting is a sort of energy imprint left on the world around us, capable of replaying itself from time-to-time, or that a ghost may actually be the lost, confused spirit of a deceased person that does not realize that they have actually died, the idea that people reported the same experiences over and over sounded a little more plausible to me.

While an anthropology major in college, I studied various folklore topics, and when you do delve into folklore you quickly find that there are themes and stories told by mankind that we all share to some degree. The finer details of the stories might vary, but people the world over certainly appear to have similar stories and see the same sorts of things. Maybe the tales of a phantom hitchhiker hailing cars in Dallas are simply modernized versions of vanishing spirits that haunted folks in the Old West.

If we concede that people are quite similar across regions and cultures, it may be only normal that when people meet tragic ends their confused spirits occasionally hang around and attempt to interact with the living or otherwise replay as an energy-charged, emotional event over and over in a similar fashion regardless of where they were live. There is even the idea that these stories are nothing more than tales told to warn generation after generation about the dangers of picking-up hitchhikers, whether living or dead, or maybe the tales are just intended to be entertaining ways of telling others to be careful traveling at night. There are several different themes that you can focus on present in any given tale.

Interestingly, Brian Haughton notes in *Lore of the Ghost* that ghostly women in white (which are similar in nature, but not exactly the same as vanishing hitchhiker ghosts) are historically and curiously much more common than phantom men dressed in white. "The most important aspect of ghostly white ladies is their association with wells, pools, rivers, fords, bridges, stiles, gates, and other luminous places. This characteristic, a common motif in ghost lore, is extremely significant as it was at such places, the boundaries between the known and unknown, between life and death, that supernatural entities were expected to appear," Mr. Haughton noted.

As for the Lady of White Rock Lake legend, there are certainly those tall tales that seem to stretch suspension of disbelief farther than others, but many do have at least a kernel of truth at their core. I think in this case, it's possible that the common urban legend of the vanishing hitchhiker was linked to one or more of the tragic events mentioned above, and that the story continued to grow and change as the tales spread.

The fact is, these stories mean something to the people of Dallas as well as others around the world and will continue to do so. I am a little skeptical, though, about those supposedly rock-solid reports of people encountering the lady of the lake. Until we have better proof to accompany these reports, I suspect we'll still be hearing about the ghostly girl of White Rock as her tale rises from the waters to capture the imaginations of Dallasites in the decades to come.

Miss Mooney,
Are You Here With Us?

At 814 Water Street is a one-story, gingerbread-trimmed Victorian house dating back to at least 1895. Since then the house has had several residents and, if you believe the oft-told stories surrounding the place several of those residents are still there today, in spirit if nothing else!

The spooky goings-on at the home first came to light around 1984 when then-owners Tom and Melissa Baker bought the property after the vine-covered home had been sitting vacant for several years. With some elbow grease and the dream of building a local restaurant that would serve up delicious down-home favorites they founded what is now The Catfish Plantation. According to Melissa it didn't take long for the new owners to begin experiencing strange happenings. Most of the phenomena seemed to indicate some sort of poltergeist activity as well as some other form of an intelligent haunting. Non-working clocks suddenly chimed, knocks were heard coming from within the walls, toilets flushed on their own, objects seemed to move around the restaurant of their own accord, glasses shattered and sudden blasts of cool air made their way throughout the place.

Initially the Bakers didn't want to let the ghost out of the bag about their new restaurant's unseen guests. Eventually Melissa contacted a radio show, which was discussing supernatural topics, and over the years that followed the restaurant has gained its fair share of publicity for both their lively ghosts and famous fried catfish. An extensive fire that broke out in the kitchen in 2003 might nearly have closed down the restaurant for good had the resilient Bakers simply cut their losses. Approximately seventy-five percent of the building lay in smoldering ashes, but after a year of reconstruction the restaurant was back in tip-top shape the ghostly experiences reported at the historic home would spark to life once more. In 2007, the Bakers sold the business to close friends Richard and Anne Landis.

On the off-chance that the restaurant was still active, I contacted manager Shawn Sparks to set up a time to visit with her, order some southern cooking, and shoot the breeze about the cold spots drifting around The Catfish Plantation.

Nick and I trekked down on a hot Saturday in August to meet with Shawn and have a late lunch. When we arrived we were told by the nice hostess that Shawn was out running errands for the "Ghost Party" they were holding at the restaurant later that night. Select Saturday nights were reserved for customers with a taste for the paranormal, something I was sure to inquire about before we left.

As we were led over into dining room "A", one of the repurposed rooms of the former house, we plopped-down at a table and perused the menu. As I'd heard stories of silverware disappearing, I promptly set one of our place settings on the corner of an empty table next to us just to see if any unseen hands might move it before we were finished eating. A friendly waitress took our orders and in no time we had more fried chicken, mashed potatoes, fried okra and iced tea than we could possibly consume in one sitting. Our waitress returned for refills and, as I looked to the empty table next to us, my heart skipped a beat — the place setting I'd set down not an hour earlier had vanished!

I quizzically turned my head to Nick with a look that elicited a quick reply. "Yeah, the silverware is gone…might have been a ghost. Of course, it was actually just the waitress that picked it up, genius. I saw it," he said, sounding a little sad for having broken the news to me.

We went up to the front cash register and closed our tab. As we waited, Richard Landis, the owner of The Catfish Plantation, stood at the register tending to some business and asked us how everything was. We struck up a brief conversation as I flipped through thick binders containing personal notes of hair-raising experiences left by guests over the years. Landis told us that he originally was a bit skeptical of it all himself, but over time and by way of some of his own experiences he had become somewhat of a believer in the ghosts that supposedly walked around the house.

Landis was a pleasant fellow and during our casual conversation he revealed that he was a veteran, a business owner, and (surprisingly) an extremely well-educated gentleman in the area of physics for a major aerospace company. In other words, he was not the typical kind of person you might expect to utter the words: "I believe in ghosts."

Shawn Sparks finally came whirling into the front door carrying a few shopping bags. She stopped to greet us and directed us over to settle down at a table in dining room "D" to talk ghosts.

Shawn was a former assistant of the ASUP or the Association for the Study of Unexplained Phenomenon, a non-profit research and education corporation focused on studying paranormal phenomena. ASUP's founding member Rick Moran, a longtime paranormal investigator and author, worked closely with The Catfish Plantation in setting up their special "Ghost Party" events.

Shawn started at the beginning, telling Nick and I about the first known owners of the property and how the home exchanged hands over the years. We listened intently to the stories of how some of the spirits met their end in the house. It grew clear that many lives had been linked to this old home.

"The next spirit that we have here is Caroline Mooney," Shawn continued. "She actually passed away December 3, 1971, and she died in this particular room — the 'blue room' here, it was her bedroom. It's listed on her death certificate as a stroke, but she was in her eighties so, you know, at that point it was natural causes," Shawn said.

"So she's still here. She's the one that's associated greatly with breaking stemware. She doesn't like alcohol being served in the building because she was a very staunch Baptist lady and she will actually try to break the glasses," she said. "If you start getting rowdy, or what she considers rowdy, she doesn't like that and she will let you know if you're doing something that she doesn't like by making things move or turning on and off the fryers. We kinda have to sweet-talk her sometimes to get her to turn fryer one back on because that seems to be the one she's able to manipulate the best," Shawn said casually.

I couldn't fathom a ghost that needed a person to "sweet-talk" her into making the kitchen stove turn back on! It would be one thing if Shawn had seen and experienced these events as a delusional shut-in, but it's quite another thing if many people had these same experiences and collectively agreed that an invisible old lady was impeding the process of getting dinner to the tables of customers!

"We'll be like, 'please Miss Caroline, can you turn this fryer back on?' We'll have to ask her very nicely and it's always 'Miss Caroline' or 'Miss Mooney,'" Shawn said.

"Does it usually work to just ask?" I asked.

"Yeah, because we'll be hitting the 'On/Off' button and nothing happens and then I guess she feels like we've had enough and she'll turn it back on. She'll allow it to come back on," Shawn replied. "She also makes objects move in the kitchen, I believe that's her. We've had cutting boards that have flown out from where they're stored. We've had fish racks come flying down above the fish sink. We've actually seen objects rise up in the air, drop straight down," she continued, pantomiming picking-up and throwing a stack of dishes to the ground.

"I was always curious, was it as if someone had just slapped them from where they were or was it like they were being..." Nick interjected, clearly interested in the blatant moving around of objects attributed to the late Miss Mooney.

"Sometimes it's with force. Sometimes it's as if someone's just picking it up and dropping it," Shawn answered. "There are different types of object manipulation that occurs in the restaurant. One of the spirits likes to cross the silverware. That's normally been attributed to Will, but we're not sure, in fact, if he does that. I've actually set every table in this room with silverware and I came back one time and every spoon was missing off of all the tables."

"Where were they? Did you ever find them?" Nick asked, leaning forward a bit on his elbows.

"I don't know... I suspect that one day we're going to actually, like, bust into a wall somewhere and there's gonna be spoons in there, because we have to buy spoons constantly to replace them. I don't know if they're in a wall somewhere!" Shawn said a bit exasperated at the possibilities.

As we continued to discuss the hauntings, the number of ghosts just kept rising. I asked Shawn how many ghosts she thought might actually be in the home.

"I've actually sat out in the front porch with the K2 meter before and asked how many spirits were here, and at that point I'd go, 'Are there two here'? Are there more than three? Yes. Are there more than five? Yes. Are there more than eight? Yes. Are there more than ten? No response," Shawn said.

"Are there nine of you? Yes. Yes. Yes. Yes."

"So there may be four that you can put a name to?" Nick pressed further.

"Well, you know, some of them could be transient — they may just come and go," Shawn replied.

"Not every house in the world or even a given town has ghosts, but if you go back far enough people have died everywhere," Nick said, which, in hindsight, was a disturbing thought to be sure!

Shawn motioned over to Richard Landis as he walked past our table, the kitchen door swinging shut behind him with a gust of air, the floor creaking a bit with each step as he walked around towards the porch.

"He's the one who saw the knife actually levitate up into the air and drop straight down. He didn't want to tell me the story at first because, you know, he's a senior systems physics engineer," Shawn said.

Nick and I laughed and thought aloud that if anyone's world might be turned upside-down when trying to wrap their brains around ghostly activity that defied the known laws of physics, you probably wouldn't have to go much farther for an ideal candidate than Mr. Landis!

"I think there's some sort of scientific explanation," Shawn replied. "It is a scientific principle that energy does not ever totally disappear, it simply changes forms. If you believe that we are beings that have energy, I mean they've been able to prove that our brain runs on electrical impulses, and if that's the place where your spirit is that energy doesn't just go away it has to change into something else." That was an interesting point and one I had even shared with Dr. Barth previously. I felt as though Shawn had shared a similar theory with me, perhaps the 'software' of the soul didn't truly disappear just because the hardware of the body eventually gave-out.

"Do you get the feeling that there's always something going on… there is always something here?" I asked Shawn.

"One of them is always here. Yes, they do come and go because I have specifically asked them if they were bound to the house, because that would make me very sad that they were trapped at The Catfish Plantation for all of eternity!" Shawn said with a genuine concern in her voice. "You know, that's very Dante… 'This is your level of Hell'... Ha! Ha! Ha!"

The three of us laughed a bit at the thought of the afterlife being a huge disappointment for anyone unfortunate enough to be stuck in a single house for all eternity, and I speak for myself when I say that the thought made me laugh as well as cringe.

"I have asked them if they were completely bound and have they been other places and they're like, 'Yes, we can go where we want to.' So that made me feel better that they're choosing to be here and not here all the time," Shawn continued.

Shawn sat there with a meter lighting up a series of little bulbs and asking questions to an invisible person or persons that may or may not have actually been there. She seemed convinced that dead people's spirits might answer her questions directly and honestly. I've seen my fair share of "Ghost Hunters" and, while I think the idea of a device able to be manipulated by unseen spiritual forces sounds intriguing, I'm not sure that there isn't some room for operator error, misinterpretation, or unexplained influence on the devices. Yet, let's just say for the sake of argument that a ghost you can't see, and have never met was there. They were a person just like you or me with a past, feelings, and motives. How would you know that the person answering you was being honest? How could you know for sure that someone wasn't pulling your chain, and that you weren't taking every response at face value because you're just happy to be having the conversation in the first place?

"I think that there are a lot of people that come here that have had experiences, and I think that many people come here because they want to, because we're open to it and don't try to hide it. I think they come here as a kind of therapy, almost like a support group," Shawn explained.

"I've had so many people come in here and say 'I've seen this in my home, my husband doesn't believe me and everybody thinks I'm crazy, but I know this is really going on.' I think it gives those types of people who, maybe, are afraid to discuss it with their family or are afraid to discuss it with other people kind of an outlet that they can go and talk about it. None of our waitresses here are going to think they're crazy — we're not going to think they are crazy. In fact, our waitresses are always very, very friendly and very open to discussing it — if they have time!" Shawn said with a laugh, knowing how busy their wait staff can get!

"So, on the one hand I do think it's therapy; on the other, I think people come because they want to believe. Some of them may have had strange things happen to them that they can't explain and they don't want to believe that they actually have them, but they know in their mind, their rational mind, that something did happen, they're not crazy. So they want to believe. Then of course you have the skeptics that want it proven to them, and they're the ones that are normally drug-along," Shawn continued with a laugh.

"Obviously people can communicate or get some type of dialogue back and forth (with the ghosts), like 'how often do you come here?' 'Can you leave here?' 'What are you doing?' 'Do you not like something?' Do you get the feeling that they notice that people dress like this, and here's what's happened to this home, or that they are kind of living in their own time and they see what they want to see?" I asked Shawn.

"That's a good question, I don't know," she replied. "I've discussed that with a lot of different people because there are a lot of theories as to whether they actually can physically see or whether they just sense your energy, you know what I mean? I'm not sure if they're living in a separate world. It sounds cliché, but do you remember that movie Nicole Kidman was in?" Shawn asked.

"Sure, 'The Others'," Nick and I said simultaneously, showing only the tip of the iceberg of our combined movie knowledge.

"She's like living side-by-side with these other people and all these horrible things are happening to her, so she's thinking her house is haunted. They're thinking their house is haunted. She doesn't realize she's dead," Shawn said. "I think that they realize they're dead, though. We've asked them, have they gone on to other places? I mean there are too many people that have brought up the fact that they are dead."

"You can't interact with them the way you have and not have them realize that's not normal!" Nick said.

"Hehe, yeah, 'why would you ask me that question?!'" I added, thinking if you asked that to someone that was living it might cause them some confusion.

I asked Shawn if the activity in the restaurant had increased over time and she seemed to feel that it had picked up a bit since 2007, when the ownership of the business changed hands. Her thinking (and Nick's) was that as the employees and customers became increasingly more accepting and vocal about communicating with the resident spirits it had actually made the place more inviting to them, causing them to wish to hang around and interact more than they may have previously.

She felt that there was more activity noticed in general, and while a lot of it was during the quieter closed hours there was always the occasionally blatant occurrence like a fryer turning-off, or a cutting board that would jump off of a shelf in the midst of a busy night. However, she thought that for the most part the ghosts seemed to like the staff, though some events might startle them every now and then, they weren't necessarily happening because the spirits were negative in nature.

"You mentioned that you've asked them questions with the K2, like how many of them are here. Do you get the sense that they know the other ones are here as well? Like they all know there's more than just them (individually) here?" I asked.

"We did have one that we weren't really, necessarily, sure if he was friendly or not. So we did ask the others if they were intimidated by him, or if he was being mean to them, and Miss Caroline was like 'hell no!' That was almost her response, it was like 'nobody's running me outta my house!" Shawn said. "I do think that they are aware of each other. I think the ones that are here interact and kinda like each other, but if someone comes in that they don't like, like they didn't like 'that' guy (ghost)…they were like, 'well he's not going to run me off', or 'he's not going to make me do anything that I don't want to do." It's that type of attitude. So that gave me the impression that they are kind of aware of each other at some point," she explained.

"That's interesting, that being from different places and times…it's almost like, 'oh, hey, you're here too, now!' It's amazing to think, that they're going 'you're the only other person here that can see me!'" I said, thinking of how that sort of might work. Supposing people that didn't know each other in life at a location were somehow potentially bonding due to their common ghostly nature over the same place they now share and once maybe loved in life.

"I wonder, too, that if somebody did come in that they didn't like, if they would kind of band together and kick them out," Shawn thought out loud.

We talked a little about what spots throughout the house were most active, and as there may be upwards of nine spirits according to Shawn, she said the activity ranges from the front yard through every room in the place, including the kitchen and bathrooms!

"Another thing that stuck out to me as interesting was Caroline. You mentioned that she was sort of this Southern Baptist, very straight-forward, no-nonsense type of person…" I began.

"If you are a very spiritual person that happens to be here and happen to be in your present ghostly position in the afterlife, knowing that you've died but are now haunting The Catfish Plantation…" I continued.

"Then you do pass on, you know? Here's someone who's really active and who believes that the day their number's up they'll just go to a place with gold cobblestone roads in the sky and men with white beards at a pearly gate. I wonder how that works, it's almost like the idea that there continues to be a psychology of someone even though they've passed on from what you've been telling me..." I continued, struggling to put a real question into words.

"Yeah, 'heaven is what you make it', or, you know, 'heaven is whatever is in your mind,'" Shawn said, much more directly than I was apparently able to do. "My theory on that is that sometimes some people don't want to go on because they are so ingrained with the Judeo-Christian ethic that they felt like that they were bad people in life, so they're going to go to hell, so they feel like they're going to stay here because they're afraid of going to hell," Shawn said.

"In the case of Caroline, I think she just really loved this house, and this was her place. She was one of the ones that I was most concerned about because she was a devout Christian, so why was she still here? Why hasn't she moved on to their place?" Shawn continued. "I think she goes back and forth, that's my idea on it. She said that she's gone to, I call it, 'the light', or wherever. 'Have you been, have you crossed over, have you seen what you would consider heaven?'" Shawn said. "She said yes, and that's good. I'm glad, so she chooses to kind of..." Shawn explained.

"To just vacation there?" I asked, with a little laugh.

"Yeah... Yeah, exactly, I guess," Shawn replied.

Shawn felt that maybe the ghosts come and go, and while some may still be intelligent and interactive with the living, they can't interact with us all of the time, or at least in the same way we know about communicating with each other among the living. So they choose to check in, interact when they choose, and go off on their own from time-to-time to other places, and possibly to be with others like themselves.

"We kind of coexist with them and they're kind of residents of the house which is why we try to be very respectful, especially when we have these other investigators come in. You know, I'm pretty clear to them that I don't want them being mean to my ghosts. I don't want them trying to provoke — they're not going to have to provoke to get them to come out and interact with them because they like to interact with people," Shawn said.

"If you're thinking of something or want to try and get (the ghosts) to try and do something, move something, show me something, obviously not like 'roll over', but is there something that people ask to happen to let them know the spirits are there?" I asked, moving a pepper-shaker across the table as an example, wondering just how interactive these spirits could be if you directly tried to communicate with them.

"Normally if you ask them nicely and in the right spirit they'll try to make it happen. Sometimes they don't do it right when you ask them to, I mean, because like you said, they're not dogs, they're not trained animals," Shawn explained.

"If you do ask if someone's here to communicate with you, then more than likely there's someone that will come out and communicate with you. Here, I'll prove it. Let me go and get my K2, I'll show you," Shawn said, getting-up from the table and exiting the room.

Nick and I laughed a little. You could feel a sort of tingle of excitement in the air. I wondered what if Shawn comes back and we ask The Catfish Plantation ghosts a question and they in turn start setting the little lights of the K2 off in response to questions? What would that mean? Would it solidify to me (or Nick) that this is all true? Could it be that easy? What if Miss Caroline herself was sitting nearby in the dining room while we talked about her as if she couldn't hear us the entire time just waiting in the wings? It was intriguing to say the least and the possibility of talking to my first dead person seemed closer, more tangible an opportunity than ever before.

A few moments later, as Nick and I sat there thinking about other questions to ask Shawn, she returned with bag in hand ready to take our conversation directly to the unseen spirits that may have been with us the entire time.

"Okay, let's see…" Shawn said, digging the K2 meter out of a bag.

"I guess I have another question. You know the K2, I've always seen people verbalize questions, but you mentioned that there are people who have had a whole back and forth conversation. Could you say that you don't have to say something out loud so much as you could be thinking of the questions?" I asked, implying that for some people maybe the ghosts are able to pick-up on thoughts rather than have to rely on hearing a person's voice.

"I normally verbalize it out loud," Shawn said, the K2 in front of her on the table. "For example, I have this lit up and I'm going to ask: Is somebody here who wants to talk to us today?"

A family with small children had since joined us in the small dining room that was formerly thought to be Miss Caroline's bedroom, presumably where she may have died in the early 1970s.

"Is there anyone here that wants to communicate with us? There are some gentlemen here that I'm sure that you've been watching who are interviewing me for a book they're writing. Are you guys okay with us putting stuff in the book? If you're okay with it, can you make my K2 light up? You guys know how to use this. If you could just come forward…" Shawn continued aloud.

The three of us sat in anticipation... Would someone answer us? Would Caroline, Will, maybe Lola or even Elisabeth show up to let us know what's on their mind? The K2 rested in Shawn's hands, a small coin inserted at the flat button to keep the meter in the 'On' position at all times. A single green bulb was lit on the left, and we waited in the hopes that the array of lights would glow left to right, signaling a change in the electromagnetic fields surrounding us, which, some theorize, may suggest the arrival of a ghost.

"Sometimes they want to, sometimes they don't. Most of the time I get better results on the porch, which is kind of strange. I've never used it in this room, actually," Shawn said, which struck me as odd. If I were here as often as she probably is I'd have scoured every room in the house several times. Hell, once a day even to see what happened! Only the sounds of the kids eating at the table behind us and the normal noises of the kitchen filled the air. The absence of a response in a moment filled so heavy with expectation was palpable.

"Do you want to talk to somebody else? Do you not want to talk to me right now? Would you like to talk to Nate?" Shawn asked.

"I'd be happy to if they want to..." I said, hoping someone would answer our invitation for a friendly chat. The lone green light on the K2 seemed to mock us, unwavering, as if to imply either we weren't important enough to speak to, or maybe nobody was home.

"Here, you hold it," Shawn said as she handed me the K2. "Okay... Nate's holding it now, would you like to communicate with Nate? I don't think he's really convinced that you guys are here," Shawn said, not far off of the mark.

Nick and I laughed, and I hoped that maybe a ghost would throw us a bone and give us a sign we weren't all just delusional after all.

"Does anybody want to come forward? Miss Caroline, are you here? Miss Caroline Mooney?" Shawn asked. "Is Will here? Is Frank here? Is Leslie here? Are you here Leslie?" Shawn continued to search for a response from any of the known resident ghosts. Yet our questions went unanswered each time. Each time a name was called, a few moments of silence, and no reply.

"Is Lola here?" Shawn pressed on.

"I don't think we're interesting enough for them," Nick surmised.

"You may not be..." Shawn replied.

"They've been in a lot of books I think, so what's one more?" I asked lightheartedly.

"We got the hand wave," Nick said, suggesting we'd been brushed off by the ghosts.

"Is Miss Elisabeth Richards here? Is Jesse here? Is... Let's see, who else comes? Della?" Shawn asked, now on the eighth individual spirit called by name. "Is Paul here?" Shawn asked. Now our ninth ghost had snubbed us.

"We can come back another time, I'm sure they'd be happy to come back down another time if you'll want to communicate with them then, would that be okay?" Shawn threw out as a possibility for a sort of ghost "rain check" on our visit.

"Nope..." Shawn said with a bit of defeat in her voice.

We handed the K2 over to Nick, thinking out of the two of us he might be the more interesting of the investigators at the restaurant today. We talked about how utterly impressed his wife Jill might be to hear that he was able to contact real-live ghosts at a catfish restaurant in Texas.

No reply. Shawn pressed on, to no avail, asking for Miss Caroline yet again. "Seems to me like nobody's around us at the moment," Nick said with some finality.

"I don't think they are," Shawn said, agreeing with Nick's assessment. "They're probably all in the kitchen!" she added, laughing and wondering aloud if the ghosts weren't possibly bugging others over in the kitchen next to us. Shawn's cell phone resting on the table rang and the K2 kicked off a few extra small bulbs of light. Nick and I exchanged glances that the device measured changes around us — those that were normal, paranormal, and cell phone in nature. Her ring tone was oddly appropriate, playing a few notes of Rockwell's 1984 hit "Somebody's Watching Me."

Nick and I mentioned that the K2 seemed to go off around the cell phone and she said that yes, it could be affected by phones and other types of devices may interfere with the meter; however, usually if a ghost was present the meter would noticeably spike in accordance with the conversation in the room rather than only faintly and sporadically spring to life. We all resigned ourselves to the fact that, at least for this trip, the gaggle of ghosts at The Catfish Plantation weren't up for meeting anyone new that day. However, Shawn did give us a little hope for a future encounter.

"The other thing is, too, that the more that you come, the more familiar they are with you, the more apt that they are to talk to you, but, they didn't want to talk to me either today so I think that maybe they're mad at me. They could just be mad at me because I'm sitting here talking to you guys... Wes gets real upset if people don't pay attention to him," Shawn said.

Nick and I left a little dejected, but certainly as interested in the prospect of talking to a ghost as ever as we discussed the visit, the great food, and all things supernatural on our drive home that day. Undeterred, I contacted Shawn a few weeks later about attending one of their ghost parties and she enthusiastically invited me to come down and walk the house with the other party guests after-hours. Would I finally get a sign from beyond the grave that I wasn't alone in one of the dining rooms? I was determined to find out.

The October night of the ghost party could not have been more atmospheric! Bold streaks of lightning filled the sky, thunderclaps sent booming echoes across the region, and my mom and I strained to see through the buckets of rain. My mom had decided at the last minute to join me on the short drive down from Dallas to see what her son's ghost book business was all about. We finally saw the brightly lit outline of The Catfish Plantation, completely decked out with Halloween decorations.

I thought a bit more about 'Miss Mooney' and some of the lingering questions I had about the possibility of ghosts being able to communicate and interact with the living. Could, for example, I ask the supposed ghost of Caroline Mooney questions about her life while still alive and living at the home that was now called The Catfish Plantation? Could whatever force (outside of my cell phone) that seemed to affect the K2 meter answer questions about this woman's life correctly? Could it answer what denomination she was? Could it answer if she'd been married? What was her last name? Could it answer correctly the color shirt I was wearing while sitting in the room? For me, it wasn't enough to get strange signals from a device attuned to pick up on electromagnetic fields and attribute those to questions that were asked, but it would make me less skeptical that people weren't possibly reading-into these "answers" from ghosts if the answers were correct over and over again on personal information Miss Mooney surely should know. I wasn't convinced that the person operating the K2 didn't somehow have an effect, whatever it may be, on the answers received from time to time.

Miss Mooney seemed a bit more interesting to me of all the ghosts. For one, she'd lived in the house, people seemed to know a little more about her personality (including religious beliefs) than the other spirits, and she was the one spirit that seemed to cause the restaurant staff the most grief in terms of tampering with equipment and breaking glasses. Caroline appeared to have truly changed the way the staff worked, causing them to change how wine glasses were stored (now confined behind a glass door in an effort to keep them from being thrown and shattered by invisible hands), even causing staff to ask "politely" for her to allow a fryer to turn back on believing the spirit had turned it off during busy working hours. It's one thing if a ghost is believed to be lingering about, but it's quite another to have to adjust how you live and work day-to-day because of a spook's ever-changing temperament.

When we arrived, my mom and I ran quickly up to the porch doing our best to stay as dry as possible despite the torrential rain. I could already see the front entrance was crowded with a few dozen men, women and children all hoping for a glimpse of the other side and some tasty fried food. I met Rick Moran of the ASUP at the door; he would be kicking off the evening with an introduction and informative overview of ghost investigations.

Small kids with video cameras darted about room-to-room, and others discussed their favorite ghost hunting television shows while admiring the mummies, ghosts, and fake cobwebs liberally displayed throughout the restaurant. Eventually the group was led into a room set-up with fried catfish bites, chicken fried steak fingers, and hushpuppies, all of which were eagerly munched on. The largest dining room was setup as a sort of lecture hall with rows of dinner table chairs lined-up filling the room. As the guests settled down, placated now with their plastic cups of beer, wine, and fried fixin's, Rick Moran addressed the audience. Guests spilled over into the nearby "Dining Room A" (including my mom and me) to listen as Rick shared the history of his organization, their methodology, and took questions from guests about his take on genuine hauntings as well as famous cases such as Amityville, which he concluded was an overblown hoax. Rick had a thorough knowledge of countless cases and his extensive experience in practical investigations made him a true expert on reported paranormal phenomena.

As he continued, I looked around the room. It was clear based upon the faces of the teens, kids, and parents in the room that all of the formalities were delaying the real meat of the occasion — the chance to sweep through the house in small groups to investigate on their own!

As I sat listening in Dining Room A, I ran a hand across my knee and down the sleeve of my sweatshirt. To the touch my clothing felt room temperature. Yet, despite this I could feel goose bumps rising on my knee and my skin started to crawl a bit from my elbow down to my wrist on my right side. My body felt noticeably a few degrees cooler under my shirt and jeans than the air around me did. I held my hand out in front of me feeling for any subtle draft or change in temperature, but couldn't feel anything. I wondered, 'Could this be a "cold spot" I was experiencing?'

By this time, Shawn had joined Rick Moran at the front of the adjacent room and was sharing the history of the house with the group. She passed around a few photos of Caroline Mooney and Lola and I couldn't help but think maybe, just maybe the two ladies might be listening in as dozens of people visited their home hearing stories about them. It's when I looked back around the room that I noticed another member of ASUP, Bridget, a middle-aged woman, was sitting at another table pointing a small hand-held device at me, staring down at it as she moved it around in my general direction.

Bridget would aim the device right at me and then point the device to my left and right all the while with a sort of frown on her face, as if she was trying to determine what the screen of the device was doing. My quizzical eyes finally met hers and she noticed me quietly rubbing a hand up and down my forearm. She rose from her chair and walked over to me whispering that she was detecting small moving temperature fluctuations in the room with a hand-held thermometer.

"Sixty-one degrees..." Bridget would say as she pointed at my knees, "...now sixty-three..." as she pointed to the side of me. "It's like I'm feeling a cold in this room, but I can't tell where it's coming from and it's not constant...just fluctuating a few degrees back and forth," she said in a quiet, faltering voice.

Good, I thought. Maybe I'm not crazy. Maybe the temperature was changing around me after all. What did it mean? I found it odd that while I felt cold my clothes didn't seem to be affected as well and here was this other person tracking slight but distinct shifts in temperature traveling around the room. We looked around the room, the high ceiling had a vent at the top that could have certainly been the cause but the temperature didn't seem to drop due to a noticeable constant breeze or draft. Outside the rain had stopped and though it was colder the source of the temperature shifts were not something Bridget or I were going to be able to track down tonight. It was subtle, yet frustrating. Supposedly ghosts often are noticed in very small, understated ways rather than as full-bodied apparitions. Was this one such instance or simply the mind connecting unrelated dots to make sense of unrelated natural phenomena?

A few minutes later and the cold that had possessed my arm and leg had slowly dissipated. Rick and Shawn's presentation had come to an end. A sign-up sheet had been passed around during the presentation and groups of five or six were assigned. As the ghost party attendees were ushered out to the front porch for desserts and hot chocolate I felt lucky to be announced as a member of 'Group One' — the first to sweep through the house. Group One consisted of my mother and I, and we were joined by a nice couple from Oklahoma, their young daughter and son, accompanied by Bridget, and led by the twelve-year-old granddaughter of the owners. The lights had been turned off throughout most of the house save a small lamp in each room. As we walked through the front doors, the anticipation of a dozen of others followed along behind us as the crowd waited for their chance to take a personal tour.

We first visited Dining Room D — Caroline Mooney's former bedroom. I had a K2 in hand and was slowly pointing it around the room. The small boy with us watched the monitor of his video camera as he also scanned the room. The young girl leading our way held her

K2 out proudly and began asking for responses. As if on cue, the lights flickered to life as if in direct response to her questions. It was clear to her and Bridget that 'Lola' was indeed with us. Surprisingly, the other two K2 meters managed to pick up nothing at all. The group took turns asking questions of Lola, who may have been lurking nearby in the dimly-lit room, and were met with the unwavering single green light of the K2 signaling no change in the electromagnetic field. The granddaughter again would ask a question and her K2 flickered to life. Apparently not only could Lola affect magnetic fields, but also isolate the effect to a single K2 meter. After several minutes of this, we adjourned and moved to Dining Room A, befuddled by the obvious favoritism shown by Lola.

Once in Dining Room A, again the granddaughter asked if anyone was with us. "Lola, is that you?" she asked. The K2 flickered vibrantly yet again, as if on cue. "Yes, it's Lola, she's following us…" she said matter-of-factly.

I walked into the next room, Dining Room B, and began to ask out loud for someone there to show me a sign of their presence and to interact with me in some way so I could confirm their presence.

"I'm here searching for spirits tonight. I'm told by the staff that you live here, or at least visit and can understand us and interact with us. I want to believe that you're here. It would mean a lot to me if you could make the lights on this little device I'm holding change. I know you can do it. You can do it for others, please let me know you're here with me," I said to the empty room.

A few moments of silence later and the others joined me, taking seats and looking around the room.

"Hi, my thumb is getting tired… Could I trade you for a few minutes to see if I get a response using yours?" my mom asked the granddaughter politely.

"Oh sure… That happens to me, too," the granddaughter replied, handing my mom her K2, which, unlike the others, did not require you to hold down a button to keep it constantly turned on.

Again, the questions resumed. Yet, it seemed Lola had even left us, refusing to answer our questions, leaving the three K2 meters as quiet as the grave. I took one more opportunity and moved back over into Caroline's room and asked out loud again for a sign that there was a spirit entity in the house with us.

"I'm trying to speak to Miss Caroline or anyone else in the room that can hear me. I'd like to know if someone is here with me. If you can see me, I can't see you. Maybe if you made this device in my hands flicker its lights that would help verify you're here," I said.

Bridget led the group out to the front doors; we'd had a good thirty minutes or so to ourselves and, as it was already about midnight, the next five groups were going to be waiting a while for their chance to find a ghost. Bridget motioned to me from across the room that it was time to give up the ghost hunting for the night.

I nodded, disappointed that I'd not received much more than the chills on my second visit to The Catfish Plantation.

"Last chance..." I said to the empty room.

Silence.

As I exited to the porch, Rick Moran asked me if I'd picked up anything and was surprised that I'd struck out on this occasion. Apparently there had been a few experiences from the guests already that night and he was sure the spirits of the house were active, which was an interesting anecdote, but not the pronounced sort of experience I was hoping for.

Despite the hot chocolate, the guests outside were cold, damp, and anxious to get their chance to get inside. As my mom and I found an empty couple of patio chairs, we sat down and shared our thoughts.

"Did you notice the meters never went off for anyone but the granddaughter?" she asked.

"Yeah, maybe you've got to be really familiar to the ghosts..." I offered.

"Maybe," she said, "but did you notice, after I switched K2 meters with her we stopped getting any responses?"

My mom was crafty. Unconvinced herself, her switch-a-roo was made not only because her thumb was tired of holding down her K2 meter's button, but also to see if the granddaughter's luck conversing with Lola was due to a more sensitive device. The results, to my mom, were inconclusive at best.

As we sat there on the cold, wet porch pondering the night's events I had the nagging feeling that something didn't quite add up. In my research it always seemed that the places "alive" with recent paranormal activity were those that actively promoted the business as a place to commune with others interested in ghostly phenomena. While I couldn't yet say that The Catfish Plantation was haunted or not haunted based upon my own personal experiences, it was frustrating to hear of events happening that week, even that same night, I myself couldn't witness and confirm as being paranormal in nature. Maybe these ghosts were a selective bunch. If they indeed are intelligent beings, people like you or me just deprived of a physical body; maybe they could pick and choose whom they appeared to. Could Lola be more interested in talking to a familiar young girl she knew well than strange guests? If so, why would she not reveal herself to the other two children in the room? If ghosts liked the attention, why not be a little more dramatic when they did

appear to give their audience what they wanted? Be proud that you're a ghost why don't ya!

I stood alone in the front yard of the restaurant recording a few notes from the night's events, peeking through the window of Dining Room A hoping to see the blurry vision of Will or Elizabeth drift through the dark rooms. The sounds of raindrops falling through the leaves of the large trees surrounding me were peaceful, calming. The quiet night air was broken again by the sound of an electronic Halloween strobe ghost several feet away by the bushes, and I looked to the side of the house at the tombstones and death carriage adorning the property line bathed in landscaping lights.

Are there ghosts still at The Catfish Plantation? I'd like to think that there are. Certainly many people have claimed to encounter them over the past twenty-five years, and I don't for one moment believe they are all lying or involved in some mass conspiracy to convince others that a catfish restaurant in Waxahachie, Texas is haunted beyond a shadow of a doubt. The only ghosts I saw were on the restaurant's front sign, on the windows, and decorated throughout the house that evening.

"Miss Mooney, if you are here, Happy Halloween," I said as I walked towards my car for the dark drive home.

Menger Hotel—1, Riddle Family—0

My wife doesn't believe in ghosts. I love her despite this. In the years Lindsay and I dated leading up to our marriage, we had managed to spend a night in more than one "haunted" hotel. We both stayed at an east Texas hotel; Lindsay comfortably sleeping in the massive antique bed as the fireplace roared while I lay awake wondering what amorphous terrors might be stalking the hallways that night. We also enjoyed a couple of evenings, while attending a wedding, at the famous Crescent Hotel in Eureka Springs, Arkansas. There too we slept next-door to what is known as arguably the "most haunted" room in the place — the site where a worker had supposedly fallen several stories and plummeted into the room headfirst to meet his grisly demise. No ghosts emerged from the shadows of the room, and she again confronted the battle lines of the invisible supernatural and still managed a restful night's sleep.

So when I received an enthusiastic return phone call from Ernesto Malacara at the historic Menger Hotel in San Antonio generously inviting me to stay in their famous "King Ranch Suite," Lindsay was excited, but not expecting anything paranormal to happen upon my visit.

"Yeah, it should be an amazing trip!" I said. "I've heard so much about the hotel over the years — it's considered to be one of the most haunted spots in Texas, if not the entire country."

"Yay!" Lindsay replied with quasi-enthusiastic hand-clapping, a beaming smile lighting up the room.

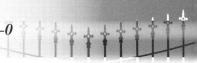

I spent the rest of the evening reading up on the Menger Hotel's history from various sources, most of which I found to reliably include a quote from Mr. Malacara regardless of the source throughout the years. A fixture of the hotel himself, Ernesto had been in the faithful service of the hotel for over three decades! As my eyes scanned various pages and websites I came across a tidbit about the King Ranch suite. Apparently it had been named after Captain Richard King, a cattle baron who created a million-acre ranch in the 1840s just south of San Antonio. Richard King stayed at the Menger often, so much so that when he finally did pass away in 1885 it was in the second floor King Ranch suite bed. His funeral services were even held in the Menger's parlors below, just over the railing outside the room that now bears his name.

Later that night, after the lights were out, Lindsay and I looked up at the darkened ceiling above our bed, chatting about our day. "That's really cool that we were invited down to the Menger," I said.

"Yeah, I'm excited for you," she said. "I want to come along, too!"

"Definitely, that would be great. I think Matt might be able to go, too," I said referring to my little brother, a Marine Corps Drill Instructor who also has a keen interest in ghosts through the years.

"Oh boy!" Lindsay said sarcastically. "So I get to go with you both? That'll be an interesting car ride."

"Well, how often can two brothers at our age enjoy a road trip to a haunted hotel? After all, he's a Marine, and if there's anyone I'd want on my side going into a building filled with enemy combatants or ghosts, my money would be on the Marine!" I said.

"Yeah, yeah…" Lindsay replied. "It'll be fun, and I may be able to meet up with a friend down there!"

"Yeah, and maybe we'll run into a ghost in our room this time around!" I offered.

"Riiight…" she again replied with more than a hint of skepticism.

"Yeah, it's named after a man that died in the bed we'll be sleeping in both nights," I said.

"Oh…" Lindsay replied, and the room felt a little bit quieter after she spoke.

~~~~~

A few weeks later Lindsay, Matt, and I loaded up Matt's F-150, bound for San Antonio. In what seemed to be a recurring theme at the time, it was again a dark and stormy night. It was well after 2 a.m. when we arrived at the empty front desk. We checked into our two rooms with a friendly hostess (the suite for Lindsay and me and a room around the corner for Matt) and headed first to Room 2052, the King Ranch Suite.

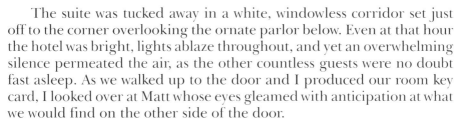

The suite was tucked away in a white, windowless corridor set just off to the corner overlooking the ornate parlor below. Even at that hour the hotel was bright, lights ablaze throughout, and yet an overwhelming silence permeated the air, as the other countless guests were no doubt fast asleep. As we walked up to the door and I produced our room key card, I looked over at Matt whose eyes gleamed with anticipation at what we would find on the other side of the door.

"Whoa, this is sweet!" Matt said as he dropped a heavy bag to the carpeted floor, walking right in as though he owned the place. "Dude, this place is freaking creepy!" he added, beaming with excitement even as the clock neared 3 a.m.

"Well, here we are!" I said. My eyes scanned the cavernous room, up along the corners of the walls that reached up towards a ceiling that had to be well over ten feet tall. The room was lined with floor-to-ceiling windows that looked out onto a balcony and the Alamo Plaza below. As I stepped around exploring the room, the floorboards beneath the carpet squeaked on occasion, adding just that extra little touch of spookiness to the empty room.

The main room had not changed much in the last century. While a small television had been added, the arrangement of the furniture appeared awkward to me, invoking an earlier time when guests would use the suite for entertaining others rather than watching a flat-screen. A beautiful old coffee table sat across from a long bench and was flanked by three lounge chairs. When looking at the seating area, I imagined a group of about seven people dressed in fancy dresses and suits retiring here at the end of an opulent dinner to enjoy a smoke and glass of brandy.

Beyond the seating area stood a tall mirror up against the wall leading out to the balcony facing the plaza. I noticed behind me just as you enter the room there was a large oval mirror positioned at a desk and regardless of which way I turned I was able to see not one but two reflections of myself which created a bit of a funhouse effect.

We were like kids in a candy store, Matt and I. He immediately retrieved the voice recorder that I brought along for conducting interviews and the occasional EVP session out of my backpack. Lindsay, however, seemed less than thrilled at our accommodations. Her eyes scanned the main seating room and then wandered over to a short, dark hallway that branched off into the shadowy bathroom and farther still the blackened bedroom.

"Well, what do you think?" I asked Lindsay.

"This place…is creepy," she muttered, and without the slightest hint of sarcasm.

"But you don't even believe in ghosts!" Matt laughed.

"Okay, maybe I don't, but I know creepy when I see it — and this is it," Lindsay shot back matter-of-factly.

"Are you going to be alright staying in here tonight?" I asked.

"Yeah, as long as you're staying in here with me! There's just something…I don't know…off about this place. I don't like it," she said in a confidence-obliterating tone. We hadn't been in our room a total of five minutes yet, and already the most ardent skeptic on all things paranormal among us was the first to admit that she would happily trade our suite for a night anywhere else but here.

"Oh, it'll be fine! Besides, what's the worst that could happen?" I asked, trying to cheer her up.

"Well, you could wake up next to him…" Matt said as he motioned to a portrait hanging on the opposite wall. I stepped over for a closer look.

"Captain Richard King, c. 1880, founder and owner of the historic Rancho de Santa Gertrudes" (King Ranch) was listed in plain black type beneath a very old black and white photo of a man dressed in a worn coat, complete with long beard reaching down to his chest and deep circles etched underneath his eyes. A no-nonsense expression on his face, as was probably reminiscent of photographs of the day, Captain Richard King was looking off to the side and in the direction of another black and white framed photo that read "Mrs. H. M. King, c. 1850" complete with a similarly dour portrait of Mr. King's wife that would send shivers up the Wicked Witch of the West's green spine.

"Huh," I said out loud, recognizing that the foundation of my own courage had a crack or two growing within it.

As a group, we progressed towards the back of the suite, turning on every available light switch along the way. First, I stepped into the bathroom, which, when bathed in light, had a yellow/white appearance and though the fixtures appeared quite modern, the shape of the space felt quite dated. The back wall of the shower was actually the same wooden shutters found throughout the rest of the suite (though firmly closed for the sake of privacy), the hard tile floor made each footstep I took echo a bit in the otherwise quiet room.

Without conversation, we moved into the dark bedroom and with a quick search found the light. The white ceiling fixture revealed where we were going to be attempting to sleep that night.

"Haha, good luck with all that!" Matt laughed as he looked upon the old bed where Captain King was said to have spent his last breaths.

A large four-post canopy bed stood imposingly before us. The lightly-colored wooden posts held a golden, bow-like canopy display above. The deep red and gold bedspread looked every bit fit for a king. The carefully carved headboard, while not fabulously intricate by today's standards must have been first-class when it was first installed in the room. The bed was offset to the right upon entering the doorway and was flanked by two mismatched night-stands on either side of the headboard. Lindsay maneuvered around the foot of the bed in measured steps, almost with a silent sense of both respect and hesitation.

"Well, it definitely looks cozy," I said, my hand grasping the nearest bedpost. The ceiling above the canopy was high, angular and the room seemed taller than it was wide giving me a claustrophobic feeling.

"How does the bed feel?" Lindsay asked, her back against the wall standing at the foot of the bed, arms still crossed.

I took a few short steps and placed my hand down on the soft bedspread, testing the firmness of the mattress. As I sat down, the wooden frame creaked loudly and a distinct crunching sound was heard as I sat my full weight down.

"Well, it's not exactly a Posturepedic," I declared as I slapped my hand a few times on the bed.

"Great," Lindsay said, her hopes of snuggling in a big, soft bed dashed in her mind.

I got up, hugged Lindsay, and patted her on the back, hoping the gesture would reassure her that everything would be okay despite her current feelings of dread. We moved into the main room and decided that since it was late this would be an excellent opportunity to roam around the halls of the empty hotel and get a sense of the place as each of us was over-tired from our long trip and would be unable to go to sleep right away.

We stepped out into the hall and took in all of the beauty of the parlor area on the second floor. Ahead of us stretched one of the main hallways, which, like many hotels around the world, seemed to look suspiciously like the ones so famously filmed in the classic movie "The Shining." It was as if all of the lights were on, but nobody was home.

To say that the main parlor was beautiful would be an understatement. White columns reaching three floors up encircled the beautiful white flooring below. A gorgeous green and blue stained glass ceiling hung majestically above. Large paintings, mirrors, and elegant benches and chairs surrounded the railing on each floor. The space caused each one of us to marvel at the sheer size and attention to detail. If Captain King had his funeral services held in this area he certainly must have been pleased at the magnificence of this part of the hotel for it surely was a breathtaking view.

Several long hallways later and it became clear that just on the second floor the Menger Hotel was a sprawling location. A total of five stories tall, the hotel is the size of an entire city block! We eventually made our way downstairs and to the main lobby, passing by old telephone booths just outside the famous Menger Bar, which is notably a replica of the House of

Lords Pub in London (a portion of the hotel Matt and I were eager to visit as it has a few of its own ghost stories as well as some top-shelf whisky).

Meandering onward, the lobby was a treasure trove of historic antiques, documents preserved behind glass, and fabulous furniture. Sure enough, an old hotel register was could be viewed in a large case set just inside the doors leading to the meticulously-cultivated open-air garden. In it, a single page of the ledger can be clearly seen, one which is associated historically with one of the Menger's ghostly inhabitants. Lindsay and I peered through the glass and there was the excerpt clear as day:

> "To cash paid for coffin for Sallie White, coe'd chambermaid, deceased, murdered by her husband, shot Mar 28, died Mar 30 / 25, for grave 7, $32.00"

Clearly not all of the Menger's history must have been pleasant. Just steps from The Alamo, the ground upon which the hotel sits was the scene of one of the most famous battles in history, what is now a shrine commemorating the brave and horrific acts that took place during a few fateful days long ago.

We walked in silence, taking in all of the details of the lobby. Matt snapped photos of anything that caught his eye while Lindsay and I held hands and drifted from one amazing artifact to the next. We eventually made our way back towards the front entrance and I found a stylish office desk with only a modest chair, a phone, and an old green "banker" lamp. Behind the desk was a plaque that read "Public Relations – Ernesto Luis Malacara."

"So that's who you're meeting with tomorrow?" Lindsay asked.

"That's the man," I replied, eager to catch up with him to discuss all of the haunted history of the historic hotel.

A quick elevator ride later and we were back in the suite. The three of us chatted a bit about what we'd seen, and still felt an air of cold about the room around us. The clock approached 3:30 a.m. and the conversation had turned to topics such as the dreary weather, what we had planned for tomorrow, and noticeably off of the topic concerning what was really on all of our minds first and foremost — the room.

Lindsay had gotten in bed and Matt had begun to dose off as the three of us retreated into the bedroom to talk a bit more, almost in an effort to avoid turning out the lights, as I suppose none of us was particularly interested to find out first-hand if we weren't the only guests present. Matt finally stood up for a yawn and stretch combo and I walked with him to the door. Lindsay sat-up in bed promptly and called-out to me to ensure that even though I was out of sight, I was within ear shot and close-by should she need me!

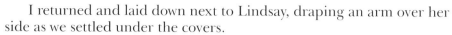

I returned and laid down next to Lindsay, draping an arm over her side as we settled under the covers.

"Are you going to turn out all of the lights?" Lindsay asked.

"Nah, I sort of want to be able to see something if it does happen," I said in a failed attempt as the chief ghost hunter on the trip to convince Lindsay that it was not because I did not want to sleep with the lights off, but because I felt it better to leave them on for the purposes of observation.

As I stared at the back of Lindsay's head so as not to have my eyes drawn out into the eerily-silent doorway and main room, I felt trapped. This bedroom just didn't seem right to me either. No full-bodied apparition had made its presence known. No disembodied voice had moaned within these walls from beyond the grave. Normally, Lindsay doesn't like to be "spooned" when trying to fall asleep, but that night I held her close and she seemed to welcome the company.

I awoke a handful of hours later. It was light out yet the lights to our suite had burned bright right through the night. I walked around in the sitting room, looked out the window at the people hurrying about in the plaza with raincoats and umbrellas and was glad that the better portion of the day was going to be spent inside. I went through the motions of getting ready as though I myself were a card-carrying member of the undead, a zombie with a pulse brushing my teeth, showering and getting dressed. Lindsay finally rose out of bed as well, and as I began to put on my boots she asked where I was going.

"I'm going to head down to Matt's room and try to wake him up," I said.

"Wait for me... I'm just going to shower off and get dressed. I'm planning on meeting Kristen in town for lunch and to go shopping today while you guys hunt for ghosts," she said.

"Okay, then I'll be right back, just going to get Matt up and moving..."

"Hey! No, wait! It'll just take a few minutes!" Lindsay said with a sound of earnest in her voice.

Later that afternoon it had stopped raining cats and dogs. Lindsay was out and about spending who-knows-how-much-on-what, and Matt and I ventured around the grounds of The Alamo. An hour or so later, we were back in the hotel lobby to meet Mr. Malacara. He extended a hearty handshake to each of us and directed us towards a quiet table next to the garden windows and a beautiful black piano. He was a poised gentleman, looking out from his glasses at us. I could see in his eyes that he'd experienced many great memories over the years at the Menger Hotel, and if there would be an authority on all related topics it would be him.

"This is a most interesting hotel, we are known as the oldest continuously-operating hotel west of the Mississippi. We are 150 years old. This structure is very, very important to the city of San Antonio. The original founder, William Menger, was a very important person in his arrival in San Antonio and obviously a man of vision," Ernesto began.

Sitting in this grand hotel lobby after taking a stroll around the place earlier Mr. Malacara's words really started to put some perspective on the historic significance the hotel has to so many people down through the years. His frank comments gave the hotel a sort of gravity, which as I would soon find out also lent a good deal of credibility to some of the more unusual events he would share with me.

"We have serviced eleven US presidents either before, during, or after they were in office, along with movie stars, religious leaders…you name it, they've been at the Menger Hotel at one time or another," he said. Following this statement, Ernesto seemed to pause (either for dramatic effect, or in what seemed more as though he was contemplating how to best preface his next words).

"Of course in addition to that we have our little…'ghost', uhm, I shouldn't describe it as 'ghost'…our little 'friends' who never leave the hotel. They checked in here many, many years back, and they never have left and I guess that they're very, very happy here," Ernesto said delicately as if doing his best to describe the Menger Hotel's "little friends" in a way that was respectful, real, and something that wasn't anything less than true…and serious in nature.

"I have often been asked by the media why there are so many apparitions at the Menger Hotel. My stock answer, though, is if I could really give you a truthful answer to that I'd be someplace else making a lot of money!" he said with a laugh. Wouldn't we all, though? As I listened to Ernesto I thought about all of the places that claim to be haunted, and while some can and do profit by associating their businesses with the supernatural very few if any have any concrete answers as to why their business is haunted.

"We have here, actually, forty-three apparitions and things connected with it. Now, I'd like to clarify one thing at the start, I'm not talking about hatchets flying through the air and heads falling off and things of this nature, but these are things that happen that are really, basically unexplainable," he said sounding a bit baffled as to how these "things" happen.

"I've named several of these, uh, of our 'friends.' I have one in particular I call "Frisky," and the reason that I call him Frisky is because he loves to put his hands on the ladies, he really does! I've had several instances here where Frisky, I guess, has made his presence known. I recall one incident, a lady who was here, she was a park ranger in a federal park, very nice lady... She said that they retired in the room late one night and they got ready to go to bed. So they got in bed, put out the lights, and went to sleep. She said that everything was quiet and all of the sudden [her old man was already snoring the minute he hit the bed] all of the sudden she said that she felt something get on the bed, and then the next thing she felt, she felt a hand being placed over her mouth and another hand pushing down on her...between her breast area...to sort of push her into the mattress. She tried to get her husband's attention as best as possible and he wouldn't wake up. She started to lift his hand, lift his arm up, and then drop it on the bed. Finally, out of desperation she rammed him in the ribs with her wrist and of course the old boy woke up then and he put on the light. When the incident was over, when the woman was actually able to talk, because a lot of these people are traumatized to the point they cannot talk for a short period of time, when it was over what happened was that they saw the imprint of two knees on the bed. That was one incident with my friend 'Frisky'."

That was it — Lindsay would never stay here another night if she had been here to hear Ernesto's story! As a recently married young man myself, I would never want such a horrible a thing to happen to Lindsay. The tale sounded sinister because it painted a portrait of something far more dangerous than a white sheet flitting-about some dark corridor spooking people. If Ernesto's tale was to be believed, and if we suppose for the sake of argument that a ghost (at least in some cases) was an intelligent being, a human spirit able to interact, even assault the living, then maybe people should take claims like these more seriously. The issue in my view was that if a man were to assault a woman in bed, defenseless in the middle of the night, and that man could be caught; he'd be dealt with as a criminal and punished accordingly. An invisible man calculating such an attack, one with the ability to simply vanish without a trace, is not something that should be brushed-off as a simple figment of a person's imagination. Ernesto stated that many people who have encountered the spirits at the Menger were traumatized for a period of time following their encounters, and whatever happened in this case in particular seemed to be negative in nature, something that a husband sleeping just inches away from his wife was somehow unable to prevent, and yet clearly physical traces in the form of knee imprints were seen by two people including the victim.

Now, could the woman have just suffered what is commonly known as sleep paralysis? It's possible; people experiencing sleep paralysis often report the sensation of a crushing weight on their chest, a sense of panic and shortness of breath, all of which could account for the woman's claims with a common, scientific explanation. However, if "Frisky's" nighttime escapades had been reported on more than one occasion, and if over the years the stories regularly revolved around female guests, while it may be a simple coincidence in which many women (potentially several of whom may not ever report such an encounter to avoid embarrassment) have attacks of sleep paralysis at the Menger, I felt it would still be wise to treat the phenomena with some respect.

"One of our better-known apparitions is that of Sallie White who was a maid…there's an interesting story in the ledger right here…" Ernesto said, motioning behind him to the hotel ledger Lindsay and I had seen earlier that previous night.

"Sallie White…lived common-law with a fellow by the name of Henry Wheeler. Mr. Wheeler had been discharged from the army; he was a muleteer in the early 1870s. Sallie was apparently a very attractive woman. She'd been married before and Mr. Wheeler, I guess, thought that she was so attractive that men would make passes at her and she may have been playing 'handsies' or whatever with them, so he was convinced that she was being unfaithful to him and as a result of that he had threatened her on several occasions that he would take her life," Ernesto continued. According to Ernesto, the couple lived just down the street a bit and not actually at the hotel.

"Well, one night he came to the hotel and they had a particularly violent argument and the legend says the woman was so afraid to go home that she went about eight blocks up the street to the old courthouse and slept on the steps of the courthouse. She went home the next morning hoping that he wasn't there but sure enough he was there and this time he had a gun. There was a terrible argument that ensued and she ran away from him and went to the area right up the street here where the fire station is. This is where the actual shooting took place. He caught up with her and shot her three times. One of the wounds was an abdominal wound, and anybody shot in the stomach in the 1870s really did not have much of a chance to survive. However, she did not die right away and of course he was taken prisoner and was incarcerated right away. The first twenty-four hours went by, and the woman still did not die, she just lay in pain. So they released him thinking she was going to live. He got out and went south and he hadn't been seen or heard from since. She didn't die until one day later," Ernesto said, laying out the tragic tale.

"The woman had no one to speak for her, and as such the hotel offered to bury her at hotel expense, which they did," Ernesto said, alluding again to the worn ledger just a few feet away, close enough to touch the ink on the pages. "I guess the only reason, and this is just a supposition on my part, that she continues to appear here is because of the fact that her spirit must have been so grateful that somebody spoke for her, because the woman had no one to speak for her at all, and someone spoke for her and buried her which is a very kind thing to do. She has been seen over a period of years, I don't know how many times, the times are countless, by all kinds of people from all walks of life. She's also always seen carrying towels. Nobody knows why…" Ernesto said. He'd heard years of first-hand stories by witnesses and was still no closer to understanding the reason behind how something like Sallie could exist the way she seemed to at the Menger.

Ernesto also shared a personal experience he had near the first floor rotunda with a heavyset woman in her early eighties, as solid as you or I, dressed in a denim-like dress with what he described as an unusual "bib" collar, steel-rimmed glasses and "absolutely the most unfeminine foot apparel" Ernesto had ever seen! Curious about the out-of-place guest, he quietly made his way downstairs to follow after the odd old lady. When he approached her and politely asked from a few feet away in passing if he could assist her he received a very odd response.

"The woman [sat there knitting] for what seemed to be an eternity, which was probably no more than about four or five seconds, at which time she looked up — and the only description that I can give you is that her eyes were just a pale…pale but expressionless blue. There was no happiness, no pain, no sorrow, no nada! Just blank. She did say, in a very authoritative tone: 'I. Am. Fine.' The manner in which she delivered these words took me to believe she meant 'leave me alone buster'! So I walked, I guess, a few feet away and then it hit me all of a sudden. It hit me — and I came back and the woman was gone. The woman was absolutely gone. Now had she gotten on the elevator, I'd have heard [the bell] and the door open. Had she gone through the doors I'd have heard the doors creaking. Where did she go?" Ernesto asked rhetorically.

He went on to tell us about an old gentleman dressed in a dapper suit and top hat that had just recently been seen by several guests in just the past few weeks in the elevator outside the restroom by Colonial Room Restaurant. The witnesses had been asked by the man upon them entering to press the button for floor "B2", yet upon motioning to press the button the hotel visitors found there was no "B2" button and turned to find the very solid-looking old man had vanished! Recently too, was a shaken-up young girl that claimed 'a ghost' had pushed her mother down to the floor, a person no one else was able to see. Ernesto wasn't immune to the occasional scare, either, it seemed. Just outside of Room 3015, the Gen. William T. Sherman Suite, Ernesto felt the piercing stare of some unseen person's eyes glaring a hole in the back of his head, a sudden feeling that swept instantly over him, causing him to shuffle instinctively to the relative safety of additional hall lighting and away from the stern-looking photo of General Sherman that still hangs there to this day.

I glanced over at Matt, with my eyebrows up, to which he shot back a single strikingly-raised eyebrow, clearly intrigued by the odd stories Mr. Malacara had shared with us. And you know what? I believed him somehow. There was a very paternal, almost grandfatherly air about Ernesto. Sure, there may have been some embellishment here and there. Good stories (and more importantly good storytellers) knew when a story was good enough on its own and when a dash of extra seasoning would make it all the more palatable. It didn't make me feel as though Ernesto would lie about all of this, or make it all up. While ghostly sightings may bring in some extra guests to the Menger, it may also turn off many others. As the public relations spokesman, Ernesto must know how to sell the hotel to folks interested in its amenities as well as its storied past, and I sensed that even though some of the ghost stories were at this point in his career well-polished I had no real reason to doubt their authenticity. Even without just a small touch of flare added to make a story more engaging, at the core of many of those stories were small events that left more questions than answers for many hotel visitors and Ernesto himself.

"You know, I've been accused… I had a disc jockey call me one time all the way from Green Bay, Wisconsin, and he said, 'You people got a hell of a racket, man, you making [this] up.' I said, 'We're not making up anything, this happens in this hotel. It does,'" Ernesto said with a firm tap of his knuckles on the table.

What about the employees of the hotel? Surely these people experienced the occasional apparition. At The Catfish Plantation, most, if not all, of the employees were fully aware of the ghosts hanging around the place and seemed very open and even positive about most of the things that happened there. However, the Menger Hotel isn't a small house renovated and turned into a restaurant: it's an enormous location with hundreds of nooks and crannies. Such a place would require an equally large staff operating at all times of the day, each and every day of the year, year-after-year, to run as efficiently as it does. So what about them? How did they feel about the ghosts of the Menger? I asked Ernesto if everyone was as certain as he was that there were ghosts in the hotel.

"The employees, of course, are used to it," Ernesto said, pausing just slightly before continuing. "I had one incident, a telephone operator who's been with us many years, and she had an experience twenty years ago in one of the check rooms in the back where an apparition came to her. To this day I have to be very, very careful when I talk to this person because if I mention that incident she starts crying."

"Wow," I said, thinking that the incident must have made quite an impression to traumatize an employee to the point they would break down when thinking back to that moment in time.

"Now why should a woman cry twenty years later..." Ernesto began, emphatically tapping a finger on the table, punctuating each word almost as if this woman's experience seemed to spur a genuine frustration and protective reaction out of him, "...after this happened if it didn't just shake-the-hell out of her, you know?" It seemed as though the stories Ernesto told were not just his alone, they were the genuine experiences shared by the people he served, the people he worked alongside of, and to doubt the tale may be one thing, but to suggest that these things did not and were not still happening was an insult not only to him personally, but also to all of the people that had related their tales to him, some of which were life-altering moments that forever changed those folks for better or worse.

"They are here. They are definitely here, and there's just no doubt about it. A lot of people don't believe this, but I think the reason they don't believe it is because they don't understand it. That's what I think actually happens. They can't fathom it so they say 'no, it doesn't exist'. It certainly does. It exists. Whether it be one day, two days, three days... A lot of people have the misconception around Halloween that we have a lot of, you know... No, ain't nobody flying around here on broomsticks and stuff like that!" Ernesto said with a slight chuckle.

Ernesto went on to say that the activity wasn't confined to one area of the Menger, but that it sprawled about the decadent hotel and no single spot could be guaranteed to not entertain the presence of a ghost at one time or another. It has become such a well-known fact (most likely in no small part thanks to Mr. Malacara himself!) that he receives e-mails and calls from people all over the world asking him about the ghosts, something that takes hours out of his schedule each week. The publicity and interest in ghosts attracted the media, amateur ghost hunters and the passing curious alike.

"I really think that one of these years we're going to be able to actually understand what this is all about. Is it going to be another area, another plane for us to go over to? Maybe it is, maybe it isn't, I don't know, but I think that one of these years that it's actually going to happen, that a lot of these things are going to be clarified," Ernesto said with a soothing tone and a welcomed sense of closure.

"There are a number of people who do not believe it and they are not going to believe it no matter what you do. It's a mystery. It's just a complete mystery why this goes on. We don't know why and maybe one of these days we'll be fortunate enough to understand it," he added.

I hoped so. When you literally feel that at nearly any moment a ghost could be doing its thing just on the other side of a wall, it becomes frustrating even at a place that is as supposedly as fertile a ground as any for the paranormal to run amok as the Menger Hotel. It's a bit like Christmas morning (albeit a potentially terrifying one) in which you're the kid lying awake in bed an hour before dawn, so eager to rush to the bottom of the Christmas tree and see what's beneath the wrapping paper. You know the presents (or in this case "presence") are there and yet you're prevented from taking a peek! What about our "presence" under the tree? What was potentially going on in the King Ranch Suite that so shook up my normally ghost-proof wife? Was there a reason for Lindsay to be concerned about staying in the room alone? If so, I had to ask Ernesto regardless of the answer. If there was something more to the suite than just an old canopy bed, what was it? Was that creepy feeling she got possibly due less to the furniture and lighting and more with something else altogether?

"There's another very interesting story on that, which concerns Frisky," Ernesto said. Already, with those few words I knew that whatever story he was about to tell would be something Lindsay would not find very comforting to hear.

"The King Ranch Suite was of course named after Captain Richard King, the founder of the King Ranch. Captain King lived here and died here and his body was held in state in that suite. I had a couple that checked in, and this is quite some time back, for a local convention. It was late at night, and I didn't get to talk to the lady for two days. Finally we were able to connect and she told me that when they arrived at the hotel, which was very, very late, 1 o'clock in the morning or whatever, she said they were assigned this room and she didn't like it and she told her husband, 'I don't like this room, there's something creepy about it'," Ernesto said, almost saying word-for-word what Lindsay told Matt and I the minute we entered the suite late last night.

Ernesto continued with the story. "She said he told her, 'Look, we've been traveling, we've been driving, taking airplanes, this, that, and the other, 'we're tired, I have a heavy presentation to make tomorrow morning. Let's just spend the night and tomorrow we'll get moved over.' So they get ready to go to bed, they hop in bed, turn out the lights, and she said everything was fine for a few seconds. Then all of a sudden she said that she saw these two faces of skeletons," he said, raising his hands to the sides of his face, gesturing at the size of the visages the woman lying in our canopy bed claimed to see. "These skeletal faces were floating about the room and smiling at her."

"So she woke up the old man and she said, 'Honey, there's these two faces of these skeletons and they're going about the room and they're smiling...', and he said, 'Look, I told you don't bother me... I've got a heavy presentation to make; I don't know nothing about no skeletons, no nothing... I want to sleep, leave me alone! Put out the light and go back to bed.' The woman said, and this is straight from her, she picked the blanket up and covered it all the way up to her neck. She said everything was fine for a few seconds and then she felt a hand (which Ernesto added extra emphasis on) on her neck, grab the cover, and slowly, just very, very slowly pull it all the way down. The woman is laying in bed, shivering, and at that point, I guess she was a very strong-willed woman, she got up, put on the lights, and told her old man, 'Look, by God, you're either going down to get me a new room now or I'm going to go down just like I'm dressed!' We met them downstairs and we moved them at 4 o'clock that morning. We did. That was in that room."

Well...crap, I thought. This was an interesting turn of events. Lindsay, if she knew about "Frisky's" other exploits according to Ernesto, and this tale in particular, would be less than thrilled about the prospect of staying in the illustrious King Ranch Suite for a second night!

"I can't tell you enough how much I really appreciate it," I said, shaking his hand.

"Let's see what happens tonight...it ain't over yet!" he said with a laugh as his eyes widened and a smile flashed across his face.

Matt and I stood at the table in the lobby as Mr. Malacara walked away. I turned and looked at Matt who was standing with his hands in his jeans pockets, grinning ear-to-ear.

"Dude, your room is freaking haunted," he replied with a teasing laugh.

"Your room is probably haunted, too, genius," I retorted.

"Oh, yeah," he said, and his smile might have just shrunk a little at the thought of the possibility.

That evening we met Lindsay and some friends for dinner on the Riverwalk. As Matt and I walked through the cold, drizzly night I told him it was probably a good idea to not mention "Frisky" at all. He agreed, and we were off for some Mexican food and cervezas. Afterwards the three of us returned to the hotel and decided to hit the bar again for drinks before heading back to our rooms for the night. We secured a small table on the first floor and began nursing a Shiner or two.

"So how was your day?" I asked Lindsay.

"It was great! How about you guys? Did you have fun chasing ghosts everywhere?" Lindsay asked in a sarcastic tone.

"Yeah, it was a great interview with Ernesto, and we had a chance to tour the hotel taking everything in. Matt may have filled the memory card on my camera with pictures of staircases and empty hallways," I replied.

"Well, we definitely need to check them all to see if I actually caught anything in those…" Matt said, hoping to find a stray orb or two.

"Definitely. Who knows, we may catch something on the camera or on my recorder in the room later tonight," I said.

"Oh boy!" Lindsay said with a faux excited glee.

"Might find more than that in there…" Matt said under his breath.

"What?" Lindsay asked, missing the comment.

I quickly glanced over at Matt, who had both eyebrows raised and a goofy smile on his face even as he lowered his head towards the table. His hands were in his jacket pockets and he shifted in his seat, slightly swinging his elbows at his sides, clearly pleased with himself. We'd had a few drinks at dinner and were on round two at the bar at that point, and already I was pretty confident that the secret we held about the other possible guest (or guests) in the King Ranch Suite might not stay a secret to Lindsay much longer.

"So, uh, let's get back to talking, then, about what everyone thought about the suite last night. Linds, you said it creeped you out, any real reason why?" I asked, trying to stay on topic while sidestepping the land mine Matt had squarely thrown out just seconds ago.

"It's just creepy," Lindsay began slowly, "like, all of the furniture…the way it was arranged and…just the arrangement of the room."

"But you don't really believe in ghosts. You've never even seen a ghost, right?" I asked.

"Right," she replied meekly.

"So, out of all of the 'haunted' places you've been, why do you think this one place is so creepy?" I pressed further.

"I don't know, just, like, a feeling. It just creeped me out," she answered abruptly. "You know, I actually thought about having to go back to the room later tonight. I don't know why I thought about it a few times, but I did. It was like I knew I had to go back there and I didn't want to. I'm glad we're in the bar, even if I'm not drinking. I don't like being in there."

"Well, you wouldn't be alone, Nate and I would be right there with you," Matt said, displaying a bit of that famous Marine Corps courage.

"Yeah, we made it through last night, what do you think would happen?" I asked.

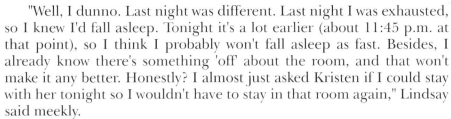

"Well, I dunno. Last night was different. Last night I was exhausted, so I knew I'd fall asleep. Tonight it's a lot earlier (about 11:45 p.m. at that point), so I think I probably won't fall asleep as fast. Besides, I already know there's something 'off' about the room, and that won't make it any better. Honestly? I almost just asked Kristen if I could stay with her tonight so I wouldn't have to stay in that room again," Lindsay said meekly.

I was surprised, this wasn't like her. Normally, she would just roll her eyes about the notion that a place might be haunted and it never fazed her before. What I saw in her eyes and the slight tremble in her voice was…disconcerting.

"Well, I'll tell you what, maybe what we'll do is hang out in the suite for a little while, then when we're getting sleepy, you and I will move over to Matt's room, and he can switch and stay in the suite tonight," I suggested.

"Hell no!" Matt instantly replied, with an incredulous look on his face. "There's no freaking way I'm staying in there by myself! Have you lost your damn mind!"

"But you're the drill instructor, remember? You want to see some ghosts? Here's your chance big man!" I said in a mocking tone only older brothers have truly perfected.

"Umm, yeah… NO, and screw you!" Matt said with a laugh, obviously sobered at the thought despite the amount of alcohol we'd consumed to that point in the evening.

"Okay, okay. Maybe Matt and I will stay in the suite together and Linds, you can stay in his room tonight…" I began before being cut off.

"Well, I'm sleeping on the sofa by the door; you get to sleep in the bed by yourself!" Matt said, quickly outlining how the sleeping arrangements were going to work. "I'm going to be near the door in case I need out of there fast!"

The three of us stared across the table at each other, jittery glances shooting from person to person as if waiting for a final plan of attack.

"What's the big deal? You guys want to find ghosts, but there might not even be anything in there at all," Lindsay said.

With that, I looked over at Matt, who was struggling with every remaining sober ounce of willpower to not tell Lindsay about Frisky. Lindsay noticed something was up, that the two of us were not being as forthcoming about all we knew.

"What is it?" Lindsay asked, flatly challenging Matt to spill the spooky beans. I looked over at him and shrugged. "Just tell her," I said.

Matt proceeded to frankly and succinctly tell Lindsay the story Ernesto had shared with us about the King Ranch Suite and the couple arriving late, the creepy feeling that overcame the woman, the skeleton faces in the bedroom, the unseen hand pulling the covers, the couple's departure from the room at 4 a.m. ... He told her all of it.

Lindsay's eyes were locked upon Matt, only briefly darting over to me to confirm whether I, too, agreed that the tale was true according to how it was relayed to us. Her arms folded, she leaned hard on them against the table, a focused look frozen on her face. When it was over, she paused for a few moments without a word, as if processing this new data in lieu of the feelings she already had about the suite.

"Yeah, pretty much," I said definitively.

"Okay... Well, I'm not staying in there again," Lindsay finally muttered, convinced now more than ever that maybe there was more than just an odd stick of furniture that may have fueled her uneasy feelings.

"As your husband, I totally am offering an out in this situation. You don't have to stay in there again," I said.

"I'm going to get you both to come up to the suite with me to get all of my things and move me down the hall, I won't walk in there by myself," Lindsay declared.

With that, we closed our tab and proceeded upstairs once again. Approaching the door well after midnight, the suite seemed to have cast a pall over us. It felt like we were lambs being led to some form of slaughter. With a swipe of the room card I pushed the door open, only to hear it thud against the wall. I flicked on the lights. The room was cold, clammy, and felt thoroughly uninviting. Every word Lindsay had said about the room raced through my mind as we looked in at the inanimate sitting room. It seemed to us as though something would happen should we choose to stay there much longer.

"I'll just get these..." Matt said, hurriedly picking up multiple bags and clothes on hangers.

Lindsay began to also pick up her things with no delay. I walked back into the bedroom cautiously. The lights had all been left on; the bed had been turned-down earlier by one of the maids. While it should all have appeared bright and cozy, there was a feeling in the air, almost the feeling you get when you stand up too quickly and the blood runs out of your face for a moment. I imagined someone just outside our periphery, someone that could see us from within the walls, someone studying us.

"Hey boss, are you ready?" Matt asked from the other room. He and Lindsay were fully loaded down with our stuff.

"Yeah..." I replied as I took a few steps backwards, my eyes slowly running along the lines of the bedroom, searching for any sign of movement. The air was swollen with a palpable sense of dread, the feeling was not unlike standing outside just as the wind dies down and a tornado begins to form. "You and I can come back in a little bit and see if anything happens."

"Okay, that's cool," Matt said.

We left the room, all lights ablaze, and proceeded to Matt's room around the corner. Without delay, Lindsay settled in and began to brush her teeth and get ready for bed. Matt's room, while it only had a King size bed in it, was infinitely more comfortable than the suite. The lights seemed brighter, the ceiling a little lower, the door much more readily accessible. It was about 1 a.m. by the time Lindsay had crawled into bed. I sat propped up in the middle of the bed and Matt lay on my other side watching TV.

"You want to go do some EVP work down there?" he asked unconvincingly.

"Maybe… I'm a little sleepy. If you want to head down there and begin, I might sleep a few minutes and then come down there to meet you," I replied, yawning through the words as they slowly fell out of my mouth.

"Okay," Matt replied.

That night we slept three-across-the-bed in Matt's room and it was restful. In the morning, I awoke early to find Matt was gone. I got up and called his phone, but he didn't answer. I showered and woke Lindsay to tell her I was going to look for him. She was able to stay in Matt's room alone, confident no boogeyman would assault her there.

As I rounded the corner to the King Ranch Suite, I saw Matt just down the empty hallway snapping photos with one hand and holding my recorder in another, talking quietly to himself.

"If anyone's here, can you please make your presence known to me?" I heard Matt ask softly as his eyes met mine and he began to walk towards me.

"Hey," I said.

"Hey. We must have been more tired than we thought last night."

"Have you been back to the suite yet?"

"No, not yet. Wanna go?"

We walked to the suite and opened the door. The light from outside filtered through the slats of the shutters and the room, while a little chilly, seemed much less ominous this morning. We left the door open and sat in the sitting room. Matt turned on the recorder and set it on the table. For the next twenty minutes we spoke aloud to an unseen person (or persons), not knowing whether anyone may have actually been listening. We asked questions about who they were. What did they want? Why wouldn't they show themselves to us? Could they make a sound? Could they move something? What was their name?

Nothing... No terrifying display. No phantom apparition dressed in period clothing. Finally, Lindsay ducked her head into the doorway and saw us; she waved her hand and sat down. I looked at Matt and called the time of death for our own little personal investigation. Upon later review of the recording I would find that just as with Bruce Hall, no disembodied voices came forward piercing the quiet white noise between comments made by Matt and I in an effort to coax a response from whatever might have been listening. Once again, it seemed that either ghosts kept their own haunting schedules or they purposely kept quiet when people were searching for them with recorders and cameras on. The same went for our photos. Matt scrolled through dozens and dozens of digital photos taken over the past two days and not even a speck of dust turned up, let alone a shadowy form. He looked over at me and shrugged.

"Nothing," he said disappointed.

We were probably not the first to visit this room and conduct a similarly one-sided interview. Many people believe that tape recorders can capture the voices of spirits. These strange sounds are called EVP or electronic voice phenomena. In many cases people don't hear anything upon visiting a haunted spot, and yet mysteriously what sounds like disembodied voices are occasionally heard when the recordings are played back. Some ghost investigators claim to hear fragments of conversations or pointed answers to questions from a person who was not apparently present at the time the recording was made.

I turned off the recorder and the three of us sat there in a moment of silence.

"This room straight up beat us," I stated flatly.

"It won Round 2; we still managed to win Round 1, so it's more of a tie," Matt said with a little bit of encouragement.

It certainly felt to me like something had defeated us that last night. At the time, the decision not to stay felt pretty damn right to us all. I'll admit, it wasn't any of our bravest moments, but what we discovered was worth it to me. Lindsay, the levelheaded, intelligent skeptic on all things supernatural, had been clearly affected by the Menger Hotel and the King Ranch Suite specifically. It scared her. It intimidated her. It did this all without anything other than a strong 'vibe.' That same vibe also got to Matt and I at some point. In some moment between coming up from the bar to the opening of that door last night, something changed in that room. Something changed in each of us. We'd traveled to the Menger to find ghosts; what we found we couldn't explain, but whatever intangible, ethereal effects the hotel cast on us was real enough.

The rational side of my mind said to me that it's just an old room in an old hotel. The furniture, to Lindsay's point, was older and arranged in a way not very conducive to what modern hotel guests may be accustomed to, and that very slight change to the feng shui may have affected us on an instinctual level in some way that has more to do with interior design than the netherworld. The suite, like many reportedly haunted places, had more of an appearance of a detailed museum exhibit than a place to catch forty winks. It was well-preserved, painstakingly clean and restored, but still it had more than just a foot firmly planted in the past. The many mirrors casting reflections, the several chairs (shorter than modern chairs), the photos of Captain King and his wife, dead now for well over a century hanging in the same room that his corpse was displayed in following his death all were things that could fuel an already jittery imagination. Most likely we've all slept in a room where someone has died without really being aware of that fact. In the King Ranch Suite, that fact is not only well-known; it's on full display for hotel guests.

Maybe the dread we had felt had more to do with completely natural stimuli our bodies were picking up that we weren't actively aware of in the King Ranch Suite. A historic location and a room designed, admittedly, in a way and with materials that were not necessarily the most modern may have had more to do with the feeling that old man King was still lurking about than we initially thought. It's certainly a solid explanation. Infrasound, for instance, is low-level sound waves undetectable to the human ear that could cause people to become suddenly uneasy for no apparent reason. The guttural growl of a crocodile or an elephant sounding others from miles away are sounds that we may not consciously be aware of, but they are definitely real and are able to travel in the space around us. Sound is similar to water, and depending on the location it can even 'pool' in areas that can send an unexplained shiver and sense of panic up our spines for no apparent reason. The Alamo plaza just outside our thick walls was a-buzz with the sounds of cars, people talking, birds chirping, and many more sounds in many more frequencies, which may have contributed to the 'ghostly' feelings we felt. I can't explain exactly how it works, only that according to acoustics experts it can and does.

However, the reality is that even if this was even part of the answer to our experiences on this trip, it doesn't begin to explain all of the other reported incidents over the years. Sound can do funny things to people, but as far as I know, it cannot pull the covers off of you or cause you to see skeletal faces dancing at the foot of your bed! The average person unfamiliar with the science of sound (and even psychology) wouldn't think about these possibilities, however. That uncomfortable feeling, to them, is best attributed to the portrait of the dead man hanging solemnly in the corner, not the running engine of the truck downstairs.

The other side of my brain that wanted to believe in the possibility of ghosts also had reasons for wanting to opt-out of a second night's stay in the suite. Captain Richard King lived there. He slept in that same bed. He died in that same bed. That couple experienced something. We felt that unseen, uneasy gaze upon us that made Ernesto (now a man in his seventies that had worked at the Menger for decades) flee the closed door to the Sherman Suite to escape the oppressive feeling that swept over him. The King Ranch Suite had only one-way in and out. Should a ghost appear in the bedroom you were either going to go through it, down a short hallway, past the bathroom, into a larger sitting room, around a corner, out the door and down yet another short hallway entrance before you'd escaped. Or, you could jump-out the second floor window to the street below as an alternative if the situation was especially dire. If it came down to a fight-or-flight scenario you'd definitely be poorly positioned for a quick getaway. You felt like the space confined and controlled you, not the other way around. Matt's room was clearly laid out, all exits easily visible unlike the suite. Once you were out of the King Ranch bedroom, you were still in the suite!

Mournfully, the three of us made one last pass through the suite and back to the bedroom. The bed was still turned down. No ectoplasm was running down the walls. No skeleton-faced ghoul was lounging on the foot of the bed. Outside, the morning sun had vanquished the horrible night.

"Wow. The maids are going to think either we're the most-tidy couple ever or they'll think we never made it back to the room last night!" I said with a laugh that lifted our spirits.

"Well, we could always say that you and Matt camped in the other room and never slept in the bed. Maybe it was an experiment you had to see if anything would move on its own in there? For the book?" Lindsay offered as one possible, plausible explanation.

"I like it!" Matt said as he high-fived Linds for the creative alibi.

"Well let's add to the mystery. Let's leave our own piece of history for the maids to find," I said.

I walked over to the bedside table, procured a pad of hotel stationary and a pen. With a final look around to make sure we hadn't forgotten anything, we turned out the lights and made our way to the door, letting it shut slowly but firmly behind us. On Captain King's canopy bed laid a single, small white tablet with a brief message scrawled in my handwriting:

Menger Hotel:

Riddle Family – 0,
King Ranch Suite – 1

The Blue Ghost

"I told you about one of my co-workers and I? Did I tell you about that?"

"Oh, no."

"A friend of mine and myself, she's in an office just fifteen feet from mine. I stepped out my door; I had paper in my hand, I was going to go copy something. She had come from around the corner and I said, 'Are you going to leave'? She said, 'Yeah, as soon as I get my purse', and I said, 'Well wait for me, I'm about to leave, too.' Now her office was in another room, but you had to go through the copier machine room to get to her office.

"We took about five steps from my office door, right across from the water fountain, and while we're…walking…heh…a man's voice, which he would have had to have been had he been somebody…"

"Uh-huh…"

"He would have had to been like a foot away from us…"

"Uh-huh…"

"And a man's voice yelled, 'Hey! HEY!' We stopped and looked at each other. Nothing happened, so she turned around and started walking again and I did, too. We took about two, three steps and it did it again — 'Hey! HEY!' And so we turned around and we started walking and we got into the copy room and I said 'Jackie…', and she turned around and said, 'What?' I said, 'Did you hear anything?' She said, 'yeah,' and I said, 'What did you hear?'

"I heard a man's voice yell 'hey' twice," she said.

"'That's what I heard, too,' I said and I told her, 'I'll meet you outside the door! So we left. There's absolutely no explanation for that. No one was there, and as we met security at the end of the pier, we asked if anyone was left on the ship and the guard said only the two of us. Nobody was down there, but she and I."

Meet Judith Whipple — historian of the Museum on the Bay and the only person I've met that works inside a ghost, 'The Blue Ghost', the *USS Lexington* docked in Corpus Christi, Texas. Her office building is an aircraft carrier roughly three New York City blocks long and nineteen stories tall. It's metal, seagulls and artifacts and it's reportedly holding much more than just museum exhibits. The Blue Ghost (speaking only of the small portion the public is actually allowed to tour alone) is a labyrinthine maze of stairs, narrow corridors, tight spaces and historical exhibits that could take the average person two to three days to tour in its entirety. That sprawling area alone is roughly only a quarter of the total ship!

Judith is the resident expert on all topics related to the *Lexington*, having been there for over seventeen years since the ship first arrived in Corpus Christi in 1992, the last World War II carrier to retire. She helps create detailed historical exhibits for the public to enjoy and also connects with former service men and women who used to be stationed on the ship. She gives guided tours to the public and preserves the rich history soaked into every inch of the aircraft carrier — and in those battle-tested nooks and crannies lurk old memories, old instruments and possibly something more.

When I visited the *USS Lexington* on a cold, overcast day in late November, the birds were circling overhead like fighter pilots waiting to descend upon their targets. It's an imposing-looking structure, haunted or not, and it had seen more than its fair share of use in battle (the *Lady Lex* sunk, shot down, or destroyed tons of enemy planes, vessels, and anything else they could throw at her!), but the carrier looked gloomy that day. You could see that the elements and events she had seen over the course of roughly seventy years had been ingrained in the ship.

It is one of the few places I'd been to that left me truly marveling at its size. This artificial island shouldn't be able to stay afloat let alone cruise the thousands and thousands of miles it did while in service around the world, I thought. It's a mobile city complete with hospitals, restaurants and an airport. At maximum efficiency it could hold upwards of 5,000 people. The sensations I felt walking the tour routes were wildly varying. One moment I could be standing on the flight deck looking out at an expansive vista of aircraft and the city skyline, an exhilarating view right up next to a F/A 18A Hornet or F-14 A Tomcat, then take a few steps away and be shocked at how high off the water I was, the wind whipping coldly around me. However, once I headed back inside to make my way towards another leg of

the tour I suddenly lost my whereabouts. Without the helpful tour signs showing me the way I would have surely gotten lost inside the intricate network that comprised the guts of the carrier.

I normally might entertain the notion that a ghost would haunt a building, but this was a location unlike any other I had encountered. Hundreds of people lost their lives here over the years via various tragedies, some in battle and others due to accidents. Surely if a place could be haunted The Blue Ghost (which received her nickname thanks to both her color as well as for famously being reported to have been sunk several times by Tokyo Rose) this aircraft carrier would be just as ideal a candidate as any other spot to harbor a spirit or two. As I approached the hanger deck from the shore I looked up and saw a black-lined Rising Sun flag up on the aft side of the island. It was at that exact spot that on November 5, 1944 a Japanese Kamikaze plane hit the *Lexington* at 250 mph, killing fifty and injuring 132 others on board that day. Taking in the enormous amount of history on display and staggered by the size of the carrier my mind quickly accepted the possibility that while a single event may not have produced a ghost here, certain events certainly had a tangible, horrific effect upon countless lives.

While we all inevitably die — some by gunshot, others by natural causes — some pass in more heroic ways than others. Those that passed while stationed on the *USS Lexington* did so while in service to their country. My brother is a Marine and I have enormous respect and admiration for what he does for the United States of America. All people in the service regardless of branch make sacrifices, as do their family and friends on whom a toll is taken while they are far away selflessly fighting for our continued freedom. My trip to the *Lexington* caused me to stop thinking of apparitions or EVPs as see-through, zombie-like beings and reminded me that the ghosts might just be someone that died, someone that was a hard-working person, someone that had a family, a profession, someone that may have suddenly been robbed of the life you and I occasionally take for granted. In my travels and conversations I'd always respected the living people that told me their tales of ghostly encounters and as I walked away from the *USS Lexington* later that day I was hit with an unexpected tidal wave of respect for the living volunteers and veterans as well as the dead that may still walk the ship's murky depths.

"When people ask if this ship is haunted, what do you usually say to them?" I asked Judith.

"Well, when I first got there, I heard some stories of course, and people would ask every once and awhile... I just thought it was a hoot, you know? I didn't believe in any of that and if anybody saw anything well I would just laugh or just turn away. I [tried] not to pay attention or encourage them because I didn't believe there was anything to it. The first five or six years every once and a while we'd hear a little story or somebody would say something, but like I said, none of us really paid attention to it," she said.

"But after listening to these people, well, it just seemed sort of strange to me that...people who didn't know each other, never met each other, and never heard 'Joe's' story, they'd come up with basically the same story and I'd think 'God, you know that's kind of odd.' It really didn't hit me until about eight or nine years ago," she continued.

"One day a visitor reported that they could smell smoke. Well, of course you don't want to smell smoke on a ship, right? So our supervisor sent two of his guys down... They went down there and came right back quite upset; they smelled smoke behind a locked door. He sent them back down because somebody else complained about it afterwards and they went down there near a refrigeration room...it was on the third deck right under my office. About ten or fifteen minutes later they nearly killed themselves running up the ladder. I mean they were really in a hurry and my supervisor said 'well go tell Judith what happened.' They smelled the smoke, too, and they went inside the door, and as they got in there the door slammed shut and the lights went out," she said.

"Well, they nearly killed each other because when the light goes out, when you're below deck and you have no light, you have nothing. You can't see your hand in front of your face and you better not move because you could kill yourself bumping into things. So the door slammed shut and they were in total darkness; they still smelled smoke and by then they couldn't even find the door because they'd lost their equilibrium and their sense of everything. Suddenly, one of the guys yelled 'look up there!' He looked up at where the ceiling was because it's pitch black, and a little white light was bobbing around up overhead. It was just bobbing around — and a voice said something. They were terrified. They didn't say anything — they were terrified. Right after the light went out, the door popped open and they left in a hurry!

"Finally the light clicked on after a minute or so and the door unlocked and they ran up to my office and they started to tell me this story and I listened politely and I jotted it down and paid absolutely no attention to it until maybe about four years later when I got a phone call from a former crew member," Judith continued, speaking quickly.

"We just chit-chatted a little bit and we hung up. A couple of days later he called me back and just chit-chatted a little; I didn't know why he was calling back, but then finally on the third time he called he said, 'I've been beating around the bush here. I don't know if you hear anything about ghosts or spirits or anything, but I've got a story I'd like to tell you.' So then if he didn't tell me the same story as what happened to those kids about four years before then," she said speaking a little bit faster.

"He was getting excited as he was telling me. His supervisor in the Navy told him and his friend to go down because one of the refrigerators might have been smoking. The smell of smoke was getting pretty strong. So they went down there to the refrigerator. They had their tools and they went in the door and the door automatically shut, of course, because it's cold and they have to keep the cold in. As soon as the door shut, it 'clicked' and the light went out. They couldn't find the handle to the door or anything so they just stood there a minute wondering what the heck they should do… just stand there and maybe the light will come back on or something. The men tried their flashlights, but both were completely dead. The smell of smoke got stronger and they heard a voice. They heard a man's voice," she continued.

"We need you," the disembodied voice said clearly through the desolate darkness of the room to the panicked sailors.

"The men tried to open the door in vain and began calling for help. Finally the light came back on. They said it seemed forever, but it was probably a few minutes. They found the door unlocked, and they ran out and left the toolbox down there. The shaken men returned to the electric shop and didn't share their strange experience with anyone else, including their officer in charge for the rest of the day!" she said.

"So, that story that I heard about four years after, our crew reported the same kind of thing and that got me thinking 'that was a little weird', but that's how I started documenting things like that," she said.

I thought to myself, while listening to Judith, much like listening to stories shared by Ernesto at the Menger Hotel, that these reported incidents were certainly odd and they each seemed to honestly believe the people who had told them their experiences and were very genuine about what they felt had happened to them. If "Frisky" in San Antonio had been the cause for countless restless nights for visitors in the King Ranch Suite, maybe the *Lexington* also had a looming specter or some residual force that occasionally manifested itself in that old refrigerator room just below Judith's office.

The problem I was running into was having a first-hand experience of my own. White Rock Lake, Bruce Hall, the Menger Hotel, and now the *USS Lexington* — all of these locations were simply massive and the odds of me being in the right place at the right time looking for the right thing seemed a much more daunting challenge than I'd previously considered. As Judith said herself even being at the Lexington for several years she didn't have her own encounter with something unusual until she had long been working aboard the ship. It was frustrating to say the least. It's not everyday that I would be able to visit haunted locales and without lots of equipment (not to mention the money and time it would take to set it all up and then analyze it!) finding a ghost and/or being able to provide some form of evidence of such an encounter was a possibility drifting farther outside my grasp.

I was starting to wonder why a ghost would want to spook people anyway? I mean really, what was the point of locking strangers in a refrigeration room only to mumble some unrecognizable message to them? What would that gain? Others I'd spoken with had their own theories about ghostly motives and maybe Judith had some ideas of her own about what these possible restless spirits were still doing hanging around The Blue Ghost.

"Well if there is something it's from somebody that's been there. I don't think spirits float around... There's not one in my bedroom, I don't think! I think, they're — and it's an awful thing to think of because these were living, breathing human beings — husbands, fathers. The thought that they still might be working...this is what I think it is. What it sounds like from how people talk and what they say is that it's like they're still on duty," Judith said solemnly.

"Do you get the sense that whatever might be there knows you're there as well? That it can see or hear you, too?" I asked, referring back to her experience hearing the man's voice.

"That was the only experience I've even ever heard anybody say anything. I don't know if they were looking at us or not, if he saw us or if we were in his space? I mean, he was right there! He would have had to have been right...right beside us, that's kind of scary!" she said, obviously at a loss as to how to explain what she'd heard.

I would imagine that hearing a disembodied voice shout at me would cause me to be a little shaken as well! While Judith tries to focus her attention on the tangible history of the *Lexington*, more and more visitors, especially over the past few years, had started coming for a brush with something supernatural. The rumors of the ship being haunted were only fueled further as The Blue Ghost began to be featured on paranormal television shows. As with other reportedly haunted places, the *Lexington* began to be contacted by paranormal investigation groups from all over the country eager to visit the ship and conduct their own nighttime tours and catch evidence of ghostly activity.

As a rule Judith made it clear that the museum is very selective about who they allow to visit since the museum's foremost goal is to preserve the past and educate people on the documented history of the ship and not the less tangible spooky moments that may occur from time to time. The community programs and the strong relationships forged with veterans and other organizations are how the *Lexington* still serves her country even to this day, but did that mean Judith and the rest of the volunteers didn't occasionally admit to being surprised by the unexpected? Certainly not. They "lost" items around the office only to find that they would unexpectedly return to the same spot later, or they would hear odd sounds they were unable to quickly explain away as the normal sounds of a ship. What was working at the *Lexington* like for them? How did Judith feel about the possibility that a paranormal investigation team might find some compelling evidence of the supernatural floating about the carrier?

"Well, I hope they don't find anything!" she said with a laugh.

"I don't think about it. When I go to work everyday I don't think I'm going to meet a spirit, or see or hear... I don't think about it. We don't think like that. If we did, we wouldn't go to work! That isn't exactly where we'd work, is it?"

I laughed at Judith's response — it was refreshing to hear someone say that they didn't dwell on the idea that where they lived or worked might be haunted or not.

"We don't think like that, and I think that if there is something there it would really be a sad situation because these people are like in limbo, they can't get out. There's life and there's death. I wouldn't want to hang in there in death..."

"Do other people who work at the *Lexington* feel the same way?" I asked.

"They must because it doesn't really frighten any of us. I'm not afraid here and I don't know of any of us that are," she said confidently.

"Almost everybody has experienced something at one time or another," she said.

Many of the employees and volunteers reported unusual sounds — crashing noises, murmured voices, lights that went on and off. As with the veteran that had called Judith to share his story, many others had reported unusual happenings on-board long before the *Lady Lex* finally arrived in Corpus Christi. For better or worse, I didn't experience anything paranormal while at the *Lexington*, but couldn't help but feel that despite this fact I'd still come out ahead for having made the trip.

"It's the chance of a lifetime," Judith concluded, hearing the awe that must have sounded in my voice. "Unless you're going to join the Navy, we're the next best bet! It's very interesting and unusual..."

Servicemen and veterans probably have a different perspective on it, but for me it was like being a kid again. It's a place that's so big, so different and has so many stories attached to it — it's that sense of awe, like 'I've never really seen anything like this before!' I could only imagine how overwhelmed the *USS Lexington* might make a young boy setting eyes on it for the first time. The planes, the guns, the 'wow-factor' is truly something to behold. The exhibits evoke not only images of what life aboard the *USS Lexington* might have been like decades ago, but also impart brief glimpses into the lives of those that were the true spirit of the carrier powering her all over the world on her various missions.

Perhaps there is something more to The Blue Ghost than meets the eye. Could a spirit cause the occasional electrical malfunction? Could a ghostly vision of some tragic event be replaying over and over again? Are the voices Judith heard spirits calling-out to the living? If they are, what were they trying to tell us? How do we know what people have heard wasn't simply a living person's voice echoing wildly through hundreds of yards of metallic rooms? Without having experienced anything spooky at the *Lexington*, and with only the vague occurrences I'd experienced elsewhere, I wondered whether I'd ever see a ghost at all. I also wondered if I'd be able to know for sure that what I encountered was definitely paranormal in nature even when I might happen upon it. For these reasons, I wanted to talk to someone that wasn't looking for ghosts, necessarily. In light of the numerous stories I'd heard to this point I needed a different perspective to make sure I wasn't just accepting that these stories were all true and paranormal in nature without considering an alternative explanation.

My journey, though, was about to take an unexpected turn.

Substituting A Question Mark for a Question Mark

When I was growing up, I spent a lot of time with my good friend Jordan. Our parents and brothers became great friends. This is the same guy that wasted away summer days on his parents trampoline, may or may not have assisted in shenanigans involving potato guns, held his composure as we once sank a rowboat in the lake, and single-handedly helped me pass sophomore chemistry. Jordan is a smart guy. He's one of more than a few of my friends that manages to comprehend certain subjects at a level of understanding light years beyond the modest grasp I may have from where I'm standing.

It was a sweltering July night and Jordan and I sat on the patio at Pat O'Brien's in New Orleans. It was the second grueling night of my bachelor party, a single weekend that would come to forever be deeply etched into the memories of the distinguished gentlemen that accompanied me to the Big Easy.

As we were sipping Hurricanes on the patio (after what will remain an undisclosed total number of alcoholic beverages consumed that day), I told Jordan I was writing a book about ghosts in Texas, and his reaction was a blend of laughter, bewilderment, and larger and larger sips taken from his Hurricane.

"Well, good luck, I don't believe any of that," he said with a laugh.

"No? Why not?" I asked.

"I just don't, there's so many reasons why… I just…no," he said more than a little amused before continuing on.

"It's just a lot of pseudoscience still, isn't it? There's absolutely no proof that a ghost is the ethereal form of a person or their disembodied consciousness flying about. Look, we're sitting in the middle of maybe what could be one of the most 'haunted' cities in the world right now. Hurricane Katrina, hundreds of years of people dying, cemeteries filled to capacity all around us, and yet I haven't seen one ghost walk by! If ghosts are spirits of people who have died, why aren't they all just roaming around the place? Why doesn't everyone see ghosts everywhere and all the time? It seems to me that what people should be testing is for some form of residue left at the location of death, at least that's testable to some degree, but like I was saying, shouldn't places that have experienced a lot of deaths be the most haunted? Think about it, Nate, wouldn't mortality rates scale with reported hauntings? If that were true, shouldn't the Fertile Crescent or places that have had people living and dying there much longer than Texas be the ones that are filled with ghosts? Do other creatures have souls? Where are all of the millions of ghost cats and rats running around on Bourbon Street tonight?" he asked, his eyes widening with more and more thoughts springing to mind.

I sat there perplexed, unable to give any quick answers. Instead, I just pressed further.

"What's so wrong about people wanting to think there's something to it? Are people dumb for not asking those types of bigger questions? A lot of people think we're all spirits inside of our bodies and that there is much more to life than we can experience or explain through our senses. What's wrong with people wanting to believe in that?" I asked.

"I don't personally believe in any of that stuff — religion, ghosts, superstitions. All of those things prey upon people who just either aren't intelligent enough to really look deeper for rational, factual answers to life or who are taken in by others because of their willingness to believe certain things because of their nature. It's sad and frustrating," he said, clearly vexed by the whole topic of ghosts and the afterlife.

"So… You don't think anything happens when we die? Like, there's nothing else? No heaven? No hell? There are a lot of people out there, some of whom I've met that seem very lucid, very intelligent that think people are, if only in really rare instances, experiencing things that they can't explain other than to simply call it a 'ghost'," I responded matter-of-factly.

"Okay, then prove it. What are ghosts? Why after all of these years have we not really ever answered that question satisfactorily? Science hasn't yielded any definitive proof and yet people pay psychics and ghost hunters and whoever else to find ghosts in the attic or talk to a dead family member. It's ridiculous, why would only humans turn into ghosts and not cows? Did Homo erectus have a spirit, or did only Homo sapiens develop this magically? If humans have a spirit or can become ghosts, then why not chimpanzees? Chimps are almost humans at a genetic level, our DNA is nearly 100% the same," he said.

It was hard to argue with him, he had a point after all. No one I'd met yet could tell me what a ghost was or why only humans seemed to become ghosts (though, to be fair I've heard of the occasional phantom dog, cat or horse seemingly reported to be romping-away in death just as in life). No one had real proof that the human spirit (or whatever the case may be) could roam around old houses at night and scare the crap out of living people.

"Well, maybe it's just faith to some degree," I offered.

"Meaning?" he asked.

"Maybe we don't have proof yet of what it is, only that there are some things we can't yet explain and 'ghosts' is the way of putting a real phenomena into words that our brains and science hasn't been able to provide an answer for. Maybe there is something to it, but maybe it's not exactly what we think it is. It could be the bleeding over of another timeline or alternate dimension from ours or some odd neurological behavior we have no answer for yet, or something else bizarre like maybe 'ghosts' are some other type of real, explainable type of energy or life form that somehow mimics humans, or maybe we're all somehow psychic in our own way and do it all to ourselves...I don't know," I rambled-off.

"Well, I'm skeptical. That said, I see what you're saying, and I don't disagree that claims of paranormal activity deserve to be taken seriously. After all, today's 'paranormal' might become tomorrow's 'normal', to your point," Jordan said, and I felt a sudden sense of a small personal conversational victory.

"BUT...these things you're talking about need to be able to pass critical evaluation, they need to be able to provide some evidence that isn't all just circumstantial," Jordan added, bringing my lofty conversational moment of victory down a peg or two.

"Nate, only you would do something like this!" he said, taking a sip of his gigantic beer.

"Do me a favor, if you're really interested and not just telling me what I want to hear then check out the CFI for me. Give the people that read your book a chance to consider the other side of this 'ghost' thing and you'll be doing them a world of service versus just telling them one scary story after another, okay?" he asked.

"The CFI?" I asked.

"Yeah, they should be able to hook you up with someone with a scientific background that investigates this type of phenomena. Go find a person grounded in science and talk to them about your ghosts. Their perspective might really surprise you and anyone else really interested in getting down to the facts and not just the fantastic," he suggested.

After my extended hangover from the bachelor party had passed and the excitement of both my wedding day and honeymoon had settled down, I decided to follow-up on Jordan's suggestion. With a few clicks I had found the CFI, short for the Center for Inquiry. And what exactly is the CFI? According to their 'About Us' page the "mission of the Center for Inquiry is to foster a secular society based on science, reason, freedom of inquiry, and humanist values." The CFI focuses their activities on three goals in particular:

1. An end to the influence that religion and pseudoscience have on public policy

2. An end to the privileged position that religion and pseudoscience continue to enjoy in many societies

3. An end to the stigma attached to being a nonbeliever, whether the nonbeliever describes her/himself as an atheist, agnostic, humanist, freethinker or skeptic.

Something in the back of my mind told me that maybe I wouldn't find a member of the CFI in the rear of some Baptist church down by Waco anytime soon. The CFI has branches across the U.S. from New York to California and even a branch located in Austin. They are a non-partisan, not-for-profit organization active in the Austin community. Among other activities, they provide "an ethical alternative to religious and paranormal world views." Via their informative website I came into contact with Clare Wuellner, the Executive Director of the Austin branch who happily invited me to discuss my search for ghosts with her on a phone call. I told Clare that I wanted to really find someone who brought to the table a healthy, skeptical perspective to the topic of ghosts and haunted places. I wanted to meet someone that was sharp, rational and that could offer me some food for thought about what else ghosts might (or might not) actually be. Clare suggested I contact internationally well-known researcher Joe Nickell as a first step, and she also left me a gracious standing invitation to visit the Austin branch to speak on the topic of ghosts in the future, an invitation I definitely wanted to take her up on!

I followed-up soon after with a call to Mr. Nickell and visited his site for more information about his background. Suffice to say, the man had been all over the world and studied strange and mysterious things during his many travels! A few weeks later and I received a voice-mail from Joe telling me that he was swamped and didn't have much time to catch-up for an extended interview at the time. Rats, I thought.

Sometime later I plopped down on the couch and fired up the DVR to find an unwatched episode of The History Channel's "MysteryQuest" show waiting for me titled "Return of the Amityville Horror." As I watched, the episode prominently featured the exploits of a researcher named Benjamin Radford, who had participated in the investigation of a couple of reportedly haunted buildings with a very rational, scientifically-based approach. I immediately Googled his name and found a plethora of information. Mr. Radford was a busy fellow, too. He'd appeared on TV in numerous places such as CNN, BBC, National Geographic, and the History Channel. He'd written literally hundreds of articles as well as several books including one with Joe Nickell on the subject of lake monsters! He was also the Managing Editor for the *Skeptical Inquirer*, the official journal of the CSI, or, The Committee for Skeptical Inquiry. Founded in 1976, the CSI had some very well-known members, including Carl Sagan and Isaac Asimov. The CFI, as it turned out, was actually an affiliate of the CSI whose own stated mission was "to promote scientific inquiry, critical investigation, and the use of reason in examining controversial and extraordinary claims."

Bingo.

As I clicked from one website to another, I found no shortage of articles and topics that Mr. Radford had weighed in on and I was surprised to find such a broad array of subjects he had studied: psychics, ghosts, haunted places, exorcisms, miracles, Bigfoot, lake monsters, UFOs, crop circles… Ben Radford was now officially my hero. To think that anyone out there had a job researching strange and unusual things around the globe made the kid in me envious. Hell, it made the 29-year-old in me envious!

Mr. Radford was a smart guy, he'd been the managing editor of the *Skeptical Inquirer* since 1997, he held a bachelor's degree in Psychology from the University of New Mexico, he was a part-time film critic…the man had even created a board game! The CSI maintained a network of people interested in many odd or extraordinary things and encouraged both research and close examination of paranormal claims and it was clear from the extensive list of references I found that Ben would be one of the few (if not the best) people to speak to in an effort to see if I (or all of the people I'd spoken to so far!) were just full of it. I sent Mr. Radford an introductory email and after a few back and forth notes hurled through cyberspace we set a time to have a call to shoot the ectoplasm together.

"One of the first things that I try to ascertain when I'm looking into cases is 'who first suggested there was a ghost here'? Given that any dwelling will have cold spots or drafts, given that all of us will lose our keys or something now and then, given that any number of things that people can interpret as ghosts are 95% of the time not interpreted as ghosts, where did this idea come from that 'phenomena A' was somehow linked to a ghost or spirit or whatever else? That's always the most fascinating part to me because examining that introduces where the ghost came from," Ben said over the loudspeaker of my phone.

"For example, in Buffalo a couple of years back, you had a family: a mother, father, and daughter. They had some unexplained, to their mind, things going on inside their house. The wife of the family went to the library and the bookstore and got a whole bunch of books on ghosts, most of it being just…bullshit! Just poorly written, poorly researched, uninformed, speculative bullshit! So she thought, 'Oh my God, you need to look at this! This author says that ghosts are sometimes mean', blah blah blah. Of course, they also watched the "TAPS" TV show and they also consulted a psychic and the psychic said 'your house is full of ghosts.' So again, there's a consistent pattern where somebody will experience something that for whatever reason seems odd, but that wouldn't be odd in another context. They look for an answer and some usually ill-informed…'ghost writer' is too bad of a pun, but somebody who just honestly doesn't know much about this topic has written a book or a blog or wherever else will sort of provide an easy answer and the person is like 'okay, I mean, this person seems to know what he's talking about, he's got a blog.' Or 'I saw him in the local newspaper last Halloween, he was walking around a cemetery with an EMF detector, he must know what he's talking about.'

"So there is this really interesting circular validation, where nobody bothers to step outside the circle and say 'well hold on here, is this really true? Is this assumption correct?' Nobody has either the expertise or the wherewithal to sort of realize there's this sort of reaffirming circle and say 'well hold on, let me take a step back, is there another perspective? Is there a skeptical scientific perspective? Is there something else that also explains this?' Instead, it's really fascinating to see how these stories circle around," Ben continued.

That certainly sounded simple enough to me, and I thought back to White Rock Lake and how potentially a single event seemed to precede decades' worth of stories. Thinking back to Jordan's point, I asked Ben why couldn't we just look for a place that had historically seen the most deaths recorded over time and investigate? Shouldn't it be incredibly haunted?

"The problem with that is that the ghost believers will always have an easy out because you have to understand that nobody knows for sure what ghosts are. I mean they've never been proven to exist. I could give you a half-dozen definitions of what ghosts are — some people think they're the spirits of the dead, some people think they're psychic projections, some people think that they're reappearing apparitions, I mean, take your pick! Because there is no operative, useful definition of a ghost that more than one or two people can agree on, then the problem is there are no rules. Let's say for example that you're assuming that ghosts are the spirits of the dead, which is pretty common. Well, by some estimates there are more people alive today than have ever died in the past, so then the question is: if each person has an individual soul then where are these new souls coming from? I mean if the population around the time of Jesus was, I don't know, two million of something, where are these coming from? If you're claiming that a spirit of a ghost will remain where a person died, other people will say 'no that's not true, it's not where a person died it's where a person lived.' So that's why, for example, you'll go into a haunted house and they'll say 'sometimes you'll see the ghost of the person who'd lived here in 1502, although, you know, he died down the road at the hospital and was buried in the cemetery down there.' It's like nailing Jell-O to a wall because nobody can agree on what a ghost is and what its characteristics are — it makes it un-falsifiable and untestable," Ben continued.

"You know, if you're going to claim that ghosts are spirits of [once] living people, then why are there ghosts of inanimate objects? There are ghost trains, there are ghost stagecoaches, and there are ghost cars. Why do ghosts have clothes? Presumably top hats and canes don't have a spirit to come back. So then other people say 'no, no, you're operating on the wrong assumption, ghosts are sort of like psychic impressions that have been left over', and so again you have hundreds of thousands of amateur ghost hunters across North America and around the world all operating on many different assumptions in terms of evidence. What constitutes evidence? Some of them use dowsing rods and pendulums and psychics, other ones don't — it's no wonder that they have such a hard time proving their theories because there is no unifying theory of what the hell they're talking about!" Ben said with a laugh.

"There's no common language to really refer to. It's like some people say 'oh it's an apparition' and then you go to a medium and they go 'well that's not what I call it, and it's something different than what you're talking about'," I said.

"Right, right. Well, I giggle when I hear these people. Sometimes I'll go to a lecture or see them on TV and there will be some 'learned expert'. His caption will be 'paranormal expert' or whatever else and he says into the camera 'well you know we've identified five different types of ghosts. As we know there's this type, this type…' and I'm like 'what the hell are you talking about?' I mean, maybe in your own little construct, there's a collective agreement on 'well as we all know there are five types of ghosts', it's like 'wow, really dude?' The problem is that this is such an arcane topic that the general public either thinks 'well ghosts are silly, this is all ridiculous, nobody believes in that', but the other side of this coin is 'yeah, of course there are ghosts'. If you look at studies, up to half of Americans believe in ghosts and everybody has there own personal story of, you know, their grandmother visiting or whatever else, so you get these sort of wildly different perspectives on it. The problem is that as in many areas of the paranormal, whether you're talking about psychics or Bigfoot or whatever else, there's no shortage of self-appointed experts. Anybody can call themselves a 'paranormal expert' or 'ghost hunter' or whatever else and the general public sees them mentioned in the newspaper or on TV or they read their website or their book and they're like… Well, the average person doesn't know any better, so basically what happens is that most people will accept the explanation provided by the first so-called ghost expert they come across and say 'this is what I read'; well, okay, but they don't sort of take a step back and try to take a look at the breadth and depth of the literature on ghosts and the theories on it, which I think would give them a much more skeptical perspective," Ben explained.

What about the increasing prevalence of new technologies and the growing number of ghost investigation groups? Why is it that despite the fact that as a culture we seem to be growing technologically at a faster and faster pace that people seem to be so entranced and interested in something so unexplained? What makes ghosts so appealing after centuries to people around the world? I asked Ben why it seemed as though as we progress our interests in ghosts seem to also be steadily climbing?

"Well, I think there are two aspects to this. The first one is, of course, they're one of the few paranormal beliefs that transcend cultures. Every culture around the world has their own stories, myths, and legends of ghosts and people who come back from the dead, spirits, this and that unlike, for example, Bigfoot," Ben said.

"The idea of ghosts is one of the most widespread around the world, inherent in the human psyche, I think, because the topic itself is very personal. You're not just talking about a chain-clanking ghost in some theater somewhere — you're talking about your dead grandmother or your father that died of heart disease five years ago whose presence you still feel. The idea of ghosts has repercussions in terms of life after death, afterlife, heaven, hell, religion, spirituality, and near-death experience, so it's really a cluster of beliefs that sort of surround ghosts. The thing is if you believe in any of those then that sort of leads you to believe in ghosts. If you believe in heaven, then sort of inherently you believe in ghosts," Ben continued.

"You believe in a spirit world," I suggested.

"Right, spirit world or some people would argue even if you're a Christian, I mean you get back to the Holy Ghost...those sorts of beliefs aren't going to be really influenced by technology. Whether we're living in the present American Southwest or you're living in the 1800s in colonial India people still deal with life and the idea that there may be more to this world and whatever else. The idea that because we're becoming a more technological society, that has never crowded out paranormal beliefs and never will because they're sort of two different things," Ben said.

"What I find most interesting is that even with the dramatically improved technology over the last few decades we still don't have a good idea of what ghosts are! This is one thing that I bring up to amateur ghost hunters now and then and they never really have an answer for, so basically we're no closer to understanding what ghosts are or if they even exist [today] than we were two months ago, two years ago, twenty years ago, two hundred years ago. The advances in audio technology, infrared cameras and digital photos — all this high-tech gear that the ghost hunters are so proud of and that they trot out that look good on camera — haven't done any good. It's remarkable that if the purpose of what they're doing is trying to find evidence of ghosts, which I would assume is their purpose, then they have completely failed. I mean they have utterly and demonstrably completely failed.

"The "TAPS" guys, the "Paranormal State" dudes, and all of the dozens and hundreds of ghost hunting groups across the country and around world...all of them have completely failed because the only evidence they are getting is marginal, ambiguous orbs and weird EVPs that can be attributed to auditory paranoia and whatever else. Yet they sort of pat themselves on the back, I mean they have this really weird standard of success — and that's one reason why a lot of the ghost hunting that goes on is completely unscientific because they set themselves up so that there's no way for them to fail. They'll go into a case and if they find evidence of something they consider unusual or strange, then they consider that to be a success, but of course, they haven't explained it. All they're saying is, 'We found something we can't explain.' Well, that's not a success! If you take your car to a mechanic saying there's something wrong with the car and the mechanic calls you back the next day and says 'well, I found something, but I can't fix it.' Dude, you failed! You're a mechanic — that is not a success! You have not done what you're trying to do. Of course, if these ghost hunters go into a place and they don't find any evidence at all, then that's not taken as a sign that there's no ghosts there — it's taken as a sign that 'well, there may be ghosts, there may not be ghosts there, there may be ghosts there, but they didn't want to show themselves, maybe the ghosts were next door while we were here'. I mean they always have some excuse, so the ghost hunters, again, set themselves up so they're in a no-lose situation. If they win they win, if they lose they win, and that's profoundly unscientific. That's not how you do investigations," Ben said.

Despite all of the spooky stories I'd heard, all the creepy happenings in old buildings reported by so many people, this guy was making a whole lot of sense. Other than an uncomfortable feeling in the Menger Hotel that even shook my own skeptical wife and an ambiguous possible cold spot I'd felt at The Catfish Plantation on a cold, rainy night, I tried to think of anything else that I'd experienced personally in my own search for ghosts. Was I looking for something else and missing things that I should have been paying closer attention to? Why did it seem as though there was no agreed-upon methodology used across paranormal investigation groups to Ben's point?

"If you take them at their face value, these are groups that are either trying to explain something for the better understanding of humanity or they're there to help people cope with and deal with living in a place. Whether it is or isn't haunted, they're trying to give them something that will allay those fears or apprehensions and yet they all seem to not want to work together for a common goal. Usually, they're very secretive and exclusive," I said.

"You're exactly right — that's another good example of why what they're doing is self-evidently not working. If you're a scientist or investigator and you're trying to understand a phenomena, you want to share your evidence, you want to work with other people. I mean that's how scientists work, even scientists who are presumably competing to make a name for curing polio or something, they work together, they share knowledge, and they try and improve the methodologies.

"I've heard some people say, 'well, you know, we help people.' Well, coming from my end of things, I've encountered many cases in which I as the skeptical scientific investigator have to come and clean up their mess. I have to go and comfort people who are scared and upset because some amateur ghost hunter gave them some bullshit about how there's a ghost in their house. I mean I've had to deal with that, so it pisses me off when I hear these ghost hunters go around saying 'well, you know, these skeptics, they're not doing any good, they're not helping people, we're providing comfort.' Well, maybe you are and maybe you aren't. I personally know many cases where they're harming people, they're actually harming people," Ben said with genuine concern and more than a hint of aggravation in his voice.

"Getting into talking about the unscientific angle to it, I mean, what do you expect? These are, I mean, the "Ghost Hunters" guys...they're plumbers! They're Roto-Rooter plumbers by day," Ben started.

"They're not rocket scientists," I interjected.

"Yeah, and I understand that comes off to a lot of people as elitist, but hold on here. Part of the problem here is that a lot of the current interest and craze of ghost hunting and amateur ghost hunting comes from the TV show "Ghost Hunters", where there has been this democratization of investigation. There's this idea that anybody with a camera or voice recorder can find evidence of ghosts. You don't need any training, you don't need any background in science, you don't even know what the gadgets do. You just have to, you know, 'can you go to Radio Shack and pick up a recorder? You're a ghost hunter!' There is a very populist appeal to that because I think in American culture there tends to be this view of science of being this closed elitist. Most people have no idea how physics or chemistry works, how their plasma TV works, and it's not that there's anyone trying to keep a secret. I mean anyone can find that out, but there's this sort of anti-scientific undercurrent and I think that TV shows like "Ghost Hunters", all of those amateur groups, that directly appeals to them," Ben said.

"It just makes it way more accessible," I agreed.

"It was interesting, I was talking to a guy who is from Phoenix and he's got his amateur ghost hunting group and I asked him 'well, who's in your group?' He's like 'well, you know we pride ourselves on our diversity. We've got a college student, we've got a couple housewives, we've got a cab driver, we've got a guy that delivers pizzas…' and I think like a security guard or computer technician, I don't know what it was. It was remarkable, and I didn't want to insult the guy, but I'm thinking 'and what do any of these people know about investigation?'

"There's a reason why if a crime is committed, there's a reason why we hire a specialist, there's a reason why we hire a police detective — it's because they're trained to investigate. Whether people believe it or not, there is an art and skill in science to investigation. That's how that works! That's why not everybody can fix a car like a mechanic and not everybody can diagnose diseases like a doctor can because these people have training and, of course, part of the problem is that there is no accredited training school for ghost hunters. What I bring to it, for example, from my perspective, I do have a background in science, I do have a background in psychology, and I have a good grounding in the scientific method and what constitutes good science and what doesn't. Randomized trials, studies, and control groups, I mean these are important things to understand if you're doing investigations regardless of what you're investigating, but again you have this sort of collective hobbyists where they sit around and sort of say 'hey, who's here tonight? Let's go get a couple beers and walk around a haunted house', and it's no wonder they're not getting any evidence.

"Basically, the way I come at this is that either ghosts exist or they don't — those are the two options. If they do exist, then whatever methods the ghost hunters are using aren't working. By definition, they are not working. If they're looking for hard, good scientific evidence of ghosts, they are continually failing to find it. So the question then becomes, 'why are they not succeeding?' Well, the best way that we know how mankind has devised to investigate and understand the world is the scientific method. That's how we build bridges, that's how we built the Internet, that's how we understand about the world, that's how we discover cures for diseases, that's how we understand about plate tectonics, take your pick — all around the world, science and scientific methodologies is the best way that mankind has found in terms of trying to understand things.

"To my mind, and of course I'm coming from a scientific background as an investigator and editor for *Skeptical Inquirer* magazine, etc., my mind is like 'well, what you're doing, it's not working so why not use science? Why not use good scientific methodology?' Again, if ghosts do exist, then that is a valid, important thing to find out. I've never dismissed or pooh-poohed the idea of ghosts or anyone who wants to go look for ghosts. I've never said that's ridiculous or that's unscientific. No, if it's a real, actual phenomenon, then people should make a serious, legitimate effort to understand it. So either these 'ghost entities' or whatever they are don't exist and the people who believe they do exist are running around getting false positives and basically, essentially sort of manufacturing evidence in their own heads for ghosts or they're doing it the wrong way. I try to leave that question open; I try to be charitable about it. I don't know if ghosts exist or not, I really don't. I'm not going to sit here and say that ghosts don't exist; you know, disproving a negative, certainly a universal negative, is impossible. I mean I can go into a specific case, a specific theater or house or place, and say that the evidence presented in this particular case for this particular ghost doesn't hold up, it's not true, but that doesn't prove that ghosts everywhere don't exist," Ben said.

Ben really underscored for me that he felt that while a great many groups out there may be sincere in their efforts, if they really objectively looked at the data, their evidence, they'd realize that they are not making much progress scientifically so much as they are just catching unusual sound recordings and odd photographic light artifacts as their 'undisputed' proof ghosts exist. It sounded as though Ben had come across many self-proclaimed 'scientifically-based' groups and found their methodologies to be lacking or unfounded. Recording evidence using cameras or voice recorders was one thing, writing up results was a good thing to do, but ultimately when those groups' grasp of scientific methodologies is called into question they aren't able to always demonstrate that their investigations truly follow a truly scientific approach. Photos of orbs, unusual shadows, and garbled voices recorded in abandoned hospitals were arguably unusual, but not arguably proof of ghosts.

"It's remarkable to me that people are still peddling EVPs when there have been scientific and skeptical explanations for EVPs out there for decades. This is not rocket science, it's pretty well consistently proven that if you play an ambiguous sound or noise for somebody and you ask them 'can you hear it saying this', a lot of people will say 'yeah, I can hear it saying that.' Of course the scientific way to go about it is to say 'we recorded this' and have 100 people write down what they hear without any prompting, no context... Don't tell them 'this was found in a little boy's room and his name was Timmy', you know, don't do that shit! That's how you determine…and you know what, if eight percent of the people who hear that hear someone saying 'my name is Timmy, I'm seven years old', then hey — run with it. That's interesting and potentially useful evidence, but that almost never happens," Ben said.

"Anecdotes don't mean anything, they're just personal stories. That's not to dispute or degrade or diminish someone's personal story because personal stories can be very powerful. It doesn't mean someone is lying, it doesn't mean they're stupid or crazy, it just means that if I run into a friend who said that she just saw Bigfoot crossing the local highway, that's interesting and we can go follow-up and see if there are footprints or whatever else, but by itself there's no evidentiary value in that unless there's some hard physical evidence. So what you find is that in all these different types of evidence offered for ghosts — photographic, audio, anecdotes, whatever else — there's this superficiality to the analysis that leads to false positives," Ben explained.

"I just told you what I think people need to do better, and now I'll tell you why they won't do it. The reason they won't take a better look at photographic evidence — and the reason they won't read up on the psychological explanations — is because that takes work. That takes effort. That is not as much fun as going out with your buddies with cameras and audio recorders and tromping around some closed down warehouse or sanitarium. Reading up on the research on the scientific aspects of it and the psychological aspects of it isn't as much fun as doing it. Again, because most people are not approaching it scientifically, they're not taking it seriously. To a lot of ghost hunter groups, it's a hobby. It's like people who get together for bowling, or model airplanes, or Dungeons & Dragons — and I'm not knocking D&D, I mean I played that! This is not a group of scientists and experts trying to understand a phenomenon; this is a bunch of friends who like to think that they're on the cutting edge of exploring the unknown with digital cameras, so they are not interested, and I don't mean this in a negative way, I mean that they are not going to take the time to read up on the actual phenomena of what's going on here. They're joining up with these clubs to go walk around cemeteries on full moons with cameras and whatever else, they're not joining up with these clubs to sit around and read up on skeptical, scholarly research on the things that can be mistaken for ghosts," Ben continued.

"Right, they're looking for the evidence, what they feel is proof. Once they find that it's almost like that just proves what they already thought," I offered.

"Right, right exactly. It's like anything else — you have to do your research. If you're trying to understand something, whatever it is, don't just go out and jump in the field without having any knowledge of what you're doing. That's not how that's done. I understand it's not as much fun, believe me. I spend plenty of time researching the history of ghosts, the history of ghost photographs, the history of spiritualism, of psychic mediums, and contacting the dead. For people who are interested in it such as myself, there's lots of material to sort of set the context and once you understand the context — once you have the historical, anthropological, and sometimes the folkloric context — of these things, that helps you solve the mystery," Ben said.

"I read up on this stuff because I find it fascinating, I find it intellectually challenging, and I think this stuff is great, but you know the average amateur ghost hunting group is not going to be reading up on the history of folklore and the vanishing hitchhiker story. It's not going to enter into their consciousness because they're going to say 'what's that have to with ghosts?' Of course the answer is 'it has everything to do with ghosts!'" Ben said with a laugh.

"I get questions like 'alright Mr. Skeptic', which I love being addressed as 'Mr. Skeptic', it's great, 'what would be evidence for you? If you're telling me that orbs aren't ghosts and this and that, what sort of evidence do you want?' My answer is very simple. If we had an EVP of a recognized person who is dead that could be validated, then that might be hard evidence of a ghost. For example, let's say a ghost hunting team went into the White House and they got an EVP of what they think is John F. Kennedy, and they say 'we had a spirit medium with us and we contacted JFK's ghost and there's a recording of JFK saying something about 9/11. It's impossible that there's an audiotape of John F. Kennedy mentioning the September 11, 2001 attack, it's simply not possible. The only way that could be possible is if JFK's ghost knew about it and communicated it. We have known scientifically-validated samples of JFK's voice. We have audiotapes of him talking, so we can compare the voice prints to known samples of what that sounds like, and if it is true that JFK's voice is referring to things that happened after his death and that can be validated through voice print analysis, I would consider that to be very, very strong evidence of ghosts. That is pretty rock-solid and I will be the first person to stand up and say, 'you know what, this is amazing.' Unfortunately, all of the evidence falls far, far below that standard," Ben said.

"All of that said, you've been to dozens of places. With your background in psychology and science and all that withstanding, being skeptical in nature and with the scientific approach you bring to it, do you ever get uneasy or just creeped out by a place?" I asked, wondering if even confirmed skeptics get spooked from time-to-time when visiting a supposedly haunted location.

"Absolutely! That actually is one of the reasons why when people tell me stories of encountering weird experiences they have I usually believe them. My answer is not 'you're crazy or you're lying to me'; my answer is 'you're probably accurately reporting your experiences as best you can', I wonder what caused that," Ben replied.

Ben had investigated a reportedly haunted house in Buffalo several years ago that had unnerved him a bit and tested his skills at identifying a cause for some of the phenomena that the occupants had reported. What he would find was that he, too, would be challenged to explain what might have been haunting the family's living room. The answer was not what even Ben had initially suspected.

"In my investigation into these people's house, the downstairs was… strangely eerie. I couldn't figure it out. It was just… There was something about it… I eventually figured out what it was, but it was just gloomy. It wasn't scary… it was just sort of off-putting or it was unsettling, and I eventually figured out what it was and it was that the walls were not white. They were painted this sort of weird, off-orangey/tan color. Even in broad daylight, even with the windows open during the daytime with the lights on, it was dark in there. It was sort of psychological… Not all people's walls are white, but for most people their walls are white, just the drywall or whatever else, and most people in most environments — whether it's their work environment or home environment — are sort of tuned to assuming that the walls are kind of white and there's that amount of light in there. In this case, the walls were absorbing light and I'm thinking 'this is weird!' Finally, it was something so subtle and I only finally figured it out towards the end and I asked them about it and they said that they'd run out of paint, but that was a case of where it was definitely something unusual or spooky, sort of almost unexplainable that was hard to put your finger on that was not quite right about the place," Ben explained.

His voice registered a hint of the surprise even now at how something so intangible yet obviously noticeable about that house had mustered its eerie atmosphere from something so everyday — paint.

"Just simply getting out of that comfort zone and going to a place that's supposed to be haunted, especially with the expectation and the knowledge, the pre-existing knowledge that there may be something there, that can often create ghosts in and of itself," Ben said.

It sounded to me like Lindsay's instantaneous attack of the willies back in the King Ranch Suite may have had much more to do with the interior design of the room after all! Had she not known the room was supposedly haunted, would she have been so on edge? After listening to Ben's own experiences, I shared with him our experience at the Menger Hotel.

"I've had people come up to me and say 'I believe there's a ghost here because I felt uncomfortable in this room.' My answer is 'I believe you when you tell me that you were uncomfortable there, but why are you assuming that it's a ghost?' I'm not disputing your uncomfortable-ness, I'm sure it's true! That is one thing that's most fascinating to me about ghosts is that virtually anything can be interpreted as evidence of ghosts — a weird sound or a weird feeling. I mean, take your pick!" Ben said.

"As a scientific paranormal investigator I'm comfortable saying 'I don't know.' I'm comfortable in saying 'I'm in this room, I don't know exactly why I feel uncomfortable, but I'm not going to leap to a conclusion and say it's a ghost.' Ghost hunters, on the other hand, have sort of the easy answer — 'well I feel weird, it must be a ghost.' It's funny to me when sometimes skeptics get accused of 'oh, you skeptics, you say you all have the answers', this, that, and the other, and I say 'no, I'm not saying I have all the answers... You're the one saying you have the answer when you say it's a ghost,'" Ben continued.

"You know, we started the conversation by sort of talking a little bit about how there's no agreed upon definition of what exactly ghosts are and what you find is that 'ghost' is simply a label for something they can't explain. It's substituting a question mark for a question mark. It's saying 'I had some weird experience' and then the next step is 'that experience was a ghost.' The problem is that doesn't answer the question. Calling something a ghost or saying that you saw a ghost, that is not an analysis, that is not an answer, that is not a solution because we don't know what ghosts are, so it's simply replacing a question mark with a question," Ben continued.

"It's strange to me when people come up to me and they sort of present something as a ghost as if that means anything, as if that's an answer. Substitute the word 'ghost' for, you know, 'framiss.' You know? 'I experienced something weird; I think it's a framiss!' Okay, I think it's a framiss, too, what's a framiss? 'I don't know, let's call it a ghost!' You can pick whatever label you want to, but without having a definition of that label it is meaningless," Ben said.

"Do you think in our lifetime that someone will get closer to defining what this phenomena is or be able to come closer to measuring it better or explaining it within, say, the next fifty or one hundred years?" I asked.

"No. I am convinced you and I will both die before anybody comes to any consensus regarding what ghosts really are and whether they exist or not. Just look at it historically — there's no better understanding of what ghosts are, there's no better evidence for ghosts today and especially given the complete track record of failure of the ghost hunter to come up with any hard evidence. Ghosts are always going to be with us. People are going to continue to see them, people are going to continue to label their weird experiences as ghosts as they always have, but in terms of coming to any sort of real understanding of what ghosts are, if they exist, I don't see that ever happening. Again, this sort of goes back to what I was talking about before — either ghosts exist or they don't. If they don't exist, then the question to my mind becomes 'why are people reporting that? Why are people labeling some experience as they see it as a ghost?' That leads to my interest in psychology and anthropology and whatever else," Ben said.

"I've invariably found explanations for the alleged ghosts that I've encountered, but that's not to say that ghosts don't exist or that I might not ever find evidence of ghosts. That's just to say that in all of the cases I've investigated I've found rational, logical, scientific explanations for what people are reporting. If ghosts exist, their existence will only be proven through good science, good analysis, and good methodology. The problem, of course, is that the better the science you bring to it, the less evidence there is," Ben explained.

"There will always be just enough evidence in orbs, EVPs, anecdotes, stories, and whatever else to fuel interest in ghosts, but there will never be any good evidence presented, is my guess, because either there are no ghosts or because the scientists and ghost hunters are doing it wrong," Ben concluded.

It was funny, I wasn't sure what I would find in my interview with Ben, but I was pleasantly surprised by how engaging his perspective was about both ghosts and ghosts hunters. It was clear after our lengthy conversation that Ben was well-meaning and not the sort of mean-spirited skeptic I was almost expecting. He laid out straightforward questions, many of which it seemed not even 'scientific ghost investigators' had asked themselves. Hell, many of which even I hadn't considered to be quite honest. Yet he wasn't providing an answer either, and in his defense, why should he? The contest shouldn't be over whose camera was more expensive or whose EVP was clearer or whose t-shirt looked cooler, but rather who was going to take a critical look at not only ghosts and how people are searching for evidence of them. The scary thing for me wasn't that there were potentially ghosts out there somewhere, but that there might be a lot of really hyped-up folks running through cemeteries at night with cameras looking for their own personal boogeyman without a compass to guide them. Ben seemed to agree that while it was healthy for people to have these experiences and want to be a part of the effort to find the answers as to what ghosts might be, they needed to look before they leaped. Ben also seemed to feel that true believers dismiss rational skeptics so quickly and yet these two groups need each other if there is ever to be agreement on what so many are actively looking for out there.

I hadn't seen, heard, felt, or been touched by my own personal 'framiss', and I was wondering if I ever would without dismissing it immediately as my own imagination or unexplainable reaction to unusual surroundings following my conversation with Ben.

That was about to change.

Voices of an Investigation

Excerpts from Freestone County Historical Museum Paranormal Activity (or something)

"Monday, November 23, the board had a meeting here in the main building. I did not come into work till Wednesday. I was very busy on Wednesday, Andy and his mom were here at closing time and we all walked out to the parking area together. Andy's mom noticed the light on in the downstairs of the jail. We had not been inside the jail for weeks (it is closed to the public until renovation is complete) and although strange, I thought I had an explanation for the light. I told Andy and his mom that the board of directors had a meeting here on Monday night and they must have gone in to look around (talking about the proposed renovation) — no big deal. We went back to the main building, got the jail keys and went in and turned out the light. When I got to my car, I called Kathleen (board member) to confirm that they had been in the jail most likely. Kathleen told me that yes, she knew the light was on, but no, they had not been in the jail. She said that when she and the other members arrived at the museum, she could have sworn the light was off. As she and the board president Don were leaving, they looked over and noticed the light on in the downstairs area. She asked Don if he wanted to go get the keys and turn it off — he replied "hell no"!!!

Lights have come on numerous times in the jail even though we had it closed to the public and we go weeks and months without going inside. Other board members, volunteers and genealogy members have been here and heard sounds as if the front door had opened, books being rustled through, whispering etc.

I have been with visitors on the grounds and re-entered the building and heard the faint sound of whispering. They heard it too.

I was with the Fairfield City administrator and another city employee. We were standing upstairs discussing bootlegging activities that went on in the county and how we could renovate the jail for a bootlegging museum. We were all standing in the upstairs corridor when we heard a voice…it sounded like a man sighing or humming.

It was brief but loud. Everyone looked at each other…asked what the heck that was and we all got out of the building rather abruptly. They both said they had always heard stories about the haunted jail, but now they believed it."

The Freestone County Historical Museum is located in Fairfield, Texas. The current complex includes four historical buildings — two early county log cabins, the Bethel Assembly of God church, a jail built in 1879, and the recently completed Bass Wing, which now houses the museum artifacts. The property surrounding these structures is alive with history — stories about bootlegging, Bonnie and Clyde… Heck, the old jail was even converted into a private residence at one point! The jail was a working facility up until roughly 1913 when it became so unsanitary that it would take great expense to keep bad men there any longer…bad men who were occasionally put to death by hanging.

There are documented hangings that took place either at the jail or the new facility just blocks away, two on the grounds and one inside the second story. Some were former slaves charged with murder, and two hangings were conducted as the final punishment for men who murdered their wives. One hanging was reserved for an especially wretched individual sentenced to death for the rape of his own daughter, but it didn't end there. Two individuals died of natural causes in the jail: one man suffered a heart attack, and another was an accused cattle thief who passed away due to pneumonia despite having been bonded out of jail.

In 1872, Sheriff J. B. Rogers was shot and killed just a block down the street by a horse thief. It was only recently suggested by a medium that in 1888 a gruesome murder took place within the thick jail walls — a prisoner was apparently beaten to death with a piece of iron by another prisoner over a gambling debt. Initially the story seemed too sensational, but the museum was shocked to learn soon after that the local *Fairfield Recorder* actually had a record of the violent event! If you were to visit the museum today, you could just imagine the cramped conditions of the place over one hundred years ago. The rusted trap door of the gallows leans mournfully against a wall out back and an unusually placed metal plate on the first floor covers what has since come to be known as "the hole" or "the dungeon" that was sealed-away long ago.

These particular stories are tragic, terrible events that left an enduring mark on the history of Fairfield for generations to come. However, it seems that the past is not content to stay dead and buried. In fact, the history surrounding the museum seemed to be reaching out to visitors on an almost daily basis.

It was a Saturday in January and the clear, sunny day had given way to a bone-chilling night. When I arrived at the museum that day I was the outsider. I didn't want to know anything about the place — not the history, not the claims, nothing. I'd prepared for other locations I had visited, but none of that changed the fact that I hadn't really experienced anything supernatural yet in my journey. I wanted to go in blind and just see what happened; the evidence (I hoped) would hit me over the head if there were any to begin with. I was there to meet the museum curator, TEXPART (the Texas Paranormal Advanced Research Team), and members of Wide Awake Paranormal. The team was well-prepared — cameras were setup in various hotspots, team members were grouped together, armed with digital voice recorders, Tri-Meters, K2s, and digital cameras. I didn't get a really spooky feeling when I arrived, but armed with my voice recorder, flashlight, camera, and a thick coat, I was ready to investigate.

What follows, in their own words, are the accounts of a few people involved with that night's investigation and their thoughts on the topic of working in and investigating a reportedly haunted location.

Sandy, Museum Curator: "I think that the rumors have been long and many, back when the museum was located in the jail. Every person that lived in Fairfield that went to school here had to go to the museum in first and fourth grade... I think they all have memories of it and it scared them, they were little going through that jail and those cabins. I think they've always had a fascination with it if they were from here."

Jimmy, Lead Investigator/Wide Awake Paranormal: "Before setting up investigations, I like to get together with people, talk with them a few times on the phone, maybe meet with them once or twice beforehand to get a feel for how they are mentally, how stable they are. There have been times that we've dealt with people that seem normal and you talk to them a couple more times and you realize something's not firing on all cylinders. In that case it does us no good to try and help them; it's only going to perpetuate whatever it is they believe is going on. Even if we went in there and said nothing is happening, they're going to believe what they want to depending on their mental state. You can tell when someone's looking for attention, and a lot of times it's that they just have a very active imagination that runs with every little sound that goes bump in the night."

Sandy: "I think it might be several things. I have a funny feeling that the museum is located on original land that was deeded for the jail. So if you had to ask me seriously, I think it is something that has been there a long time and probably feels comfortable with the way everything looks, like it's familiar to a lot of the old stuff that's there. There have been some horrible deaths on the property: there has been four hangings, but you know they were just human beings, too, before they died. So maybe they're clinging on, maybe they don't know they're dead, I mean that's what I kind of feel and it might not be just one. There might be… I get the feeling that there are several different ones there, and I know that sounds weird."

Jimmy: "The first thing they told me was about all of the tapping and stuff that goes on in the museum. Now I did hear a lot of tapping, but I also had to consider all of the squirrels, pecan trees outside, any rodents in the museum… Sandy didn't necessarily want to hear that, but you have to tell them that. For one thing, if they're really concerned about it and frightened over it that gives them some sort of peace of mind. It does them no good if we're not honest with them about what happened. There are so many things that can be explained, but I'm happy for them and I'm happy for us as a paranormal team looking for this type of stuff that [following the investigation] we got some of the things that we did."

JJ, Founder of TEXPART: "TEXPART's biggest approach to things is education and verification. It's highly unusual to find anything that is as horrible as people think. Our goal is to get them comfortable with their environment. That's really what investigating is about… It's about trying to help the clients see all aspects, because you can't just think inside of a box — you have to think outside the box. With paranormal activity there is no concrete way to gather evidence."

Chrissy, new team member for Wide Awake Paranormal: "I've been looking for quite a long time for a group to join. Some of the other people I've met it just wasn't for me — the types of personalities and the way they did things — so I just never went out with anybody else. I'm more into the scientific side of it. It just worked out great."

Sandy: "We will be in there and we will hear stuff and there will be someone in the gallery looking around and they won't hear it because they don't know the sounds of the building and so they just assume that somebody else is in the back room or they assume someone is in the bathroom and they're hearing noises or whatever, but she

[Kaycee, a museum employee] and I will look right at each other and kinda go 'Mm-K'. I'm comfortable to a point and then I can go over that threshold and my imagination can get away with me like with the time I heard the footsteps going up the back stairs and down the back stairs and nobody was there."

JJ: "I get a lot of young people who want to be investigators because it's cool, it's "Ghost Hunters"! I tell them, you know, two percent of the cases we get some form of evidence and out of that two percent, one percent can be debunked. So you're sitting there after 150 cases with one possibility and that is the way it is."

Jimmy: "The worst thing that I think could happen to a group as a whole would be to get in front of a client and say 'hey, we got this' only to have the client or somebody from outside say 'no that's me' when we're really excited about a piece of evidence. If you don't go over your evidence with a fine-tooth comb you're really cheating yourself just as much as the client. We really need to take into consideration every possible angle."

Chrissy: "I don't believe fully in ghosts, I don't believe in psychics, so it's just one of those things in which I disbelieve something, but it doesn't mean that I'm not open to the truth if it's out there. I've always been raised that way and I've had a few personal experiences in my life that I just could not explain that told me that there has got to be something more. I was never taught that this 'one way' was the way to believe or this one religion is the way that you have to worship so I've always been open to pretty much anything and everything as long as it doesn't harm anybody. It's more of a question of 'does anything exist after this life'?"

Sandy: "In one way I know that I'll probably get a lot of resistance. I don't want to influence anybody, if they don't believe in it, they don't believe in it and that's OK, come for the historical aspects, we have plenty of history. You know, years ago you wouldn't have heard the word 'green travel' or 'green tourism' or agritourism, but people are trying to connect to farms now because they're about three generations now off of a farm and so they actually have to pay to have that experience. I kinda feel that's the same way with, I guess I want to call it 'paranormal tourism.' People are about three generations off from living in family homes. It used to be that you'd have a house for a hundred years in a family, now you don't. Old-timers, I think they believe in the paranormal because so many of those that you talk to say 'Oh well you know my mother came and said goodbye to me' or 'My grandfather told me not to worry when he died', you know, after he'd been dead. I think they lived with it and I think now days everybody is so transient, and again it's just like paying to go like touch a donkey on a farm! I think places like the museum, it's going to benefit from people that are interested in that because unfortunately kids don't want to go just for the history but you can get them hooked on history if you bring in some kind of excitement and this is just one way to do that."

Jimmy: "Going into this one after the walk-through I thought that there was potential here, but at the same time when it was all said and done we probably weren't going to get much. That was just my gut feeling on it. When we [initially] went through the jail we heard an audible voice of a man, that did surprise me a bit and I thought well maybe there's something here residual or something like that."

JJ: "The thing that I would really like to do is clarify something in that ghost hunting, or what we prefer to call 'paranormal investigation', is not an open-and-shut 'here's-how-you-catch-a-ghost' sort of situation. Paranormal investigation requires 'paranormal thought'. In plain words, we're using static balls, we're using toys, we're using K2s, we use dowsing rods… We are trying to do a careful observation of what might respond given a certain stimulus. We are just trying to think outside of the box for an unusual job."

Chrissy: "I think for me to truly believe in something it kind of has to hit me over the head. It's got to be one of those that there's no other explanation ever possible, which is probably one-in-a-million, and I understand that. I believe that people may experience things that to them are very real and I'll never want to say that they didn't see that or didn't hear that because I don't know. I don't have their senses, I don't have their background."

Jimmy: "The history of it is what intrigues me the most. The story behind the people there, what took place at the site. What causes residual hauntings? You know, like a tape player over and over, that's what I'd really like to understand, what is it about that particular area or event that caused it to play over and over? In studying some of that, 'residual' doesn't mean it's an everyday occurrence at a certain time, it could be years apart at the same time periodically just happening and there is no set specific day or date. That's got my curiosity piqued almost more than what we consider 'intelligent' or interaction. I want

to know the science of it, and there is a science to it. Whether people want to believe that or not there is."

Sandy: "There are people that are resistant, and what's so funny is [these are the same types of people] that tell me stories about the paranormal activity in their house! Yet they have a resistance to the museum getting publicity for that — and I wasn't just trying to just get publicity for it, I'm really trying to find out what's going on. If we do end up having special 'haunted tours' or whatever it might be, I want to be sure that we have documentation and not just say it's got activity when it doesn't."

JJ: "Whether you believe it or not, come on, we're not the only ones in the world. There has to be something beyond this, there has to be. It's just a matter of time before people realize that it's not a bad thing to believe in ghosts and spirits. It's a bad thing to ignore them or think they'll go away or treat them like some hideous monster without finding-out what's really going on. Most things are just human error. Most things are just the thought that everything that goes bump-in-the-night is a ghost when really it's something very explainable. People, when they get scared they just don't think straight and they need somebody to come in and help them and you can't do it by being rude and you can't do it by being a know-it-all or being a 'see-I-told-you-so', you've got to be able to approach it from a point of view where they can understand it. People like Chrissy. Chrissy is a new member and what struck me most about her are her kind nature, her ability to care, and her openness to try what she needs to do without being scared of it. Really that's what we look for is the person that's not afraid to do things, but that also knows how to handle the client situation and be empathetic with what they're looking for. We do care. Most of us in our group have had experiences that we could not explain. We're more sympathetic to listen to people who think they have something going on and maybe help them resolve whatever it is thus saving the need for them to feel like they need to move or that they can't sleep in their room anymore and they've got to go sleep in their truck — you can contact TEXPART because we have people that care to help you find out what it is that's bothering you. It's more than just a hobby to us. That's always been my goal is to stay people-oriented."

Jimmy: "I think that was probably one of the neat experiences; it's not just Sandy, but council members that sat down and took time out and told us the things that happened there as well. It's easy to read this stuff in a book sometimes or hear about it, but when you're there with a person talking face to face I think that lends a lot to it. The people that were involved in this whole process as well…if I were just driving through Freestone County in Fairfield, I think there's only 18,000 people in the entire county if I'm not mistaken, I'd think it was just another country town. When you sit down and realize just because these people are out here it doesn't mean that they're [making this all up], some of them are very well-educated, they're credible with what they see or hear, the things that they're telling you — they honestly believe that something's going on. For them to take the time that they did — I'm talking about the city manager, former and current city council members, former museum volunteers, historical experts come out and tell you these different things that have happened — it says a lot to me for them as people, for one thing, to admit it and then go on record about it."

Chrissy: "Those people who are scared to death because they're experiencing something, we come in and prove 'oh, look it's your wiring' or it's this or that, we can help them go on with that. Just because something odd happens doesn't mean that it's paranormal. There are tons and tons of explanations for why things happen. That one very small percent where you find out that yes there really is something as yet unexplained happening, what can you do about it? Well, what do you want to do about it?"

Jimmy: "We want to get people to learn about it…to get people to go out and see exactly what goes on, what goes into it, not just in what we do but also the people that are involved on the other side. The people that live at the home, that run the business… That's one thing I really enjoyed about this investigation. It's not always like that where the community as a whole is really interested in what's going on and not just about the haunting, but also the museum. The people involved — these people's lives — are intertwined with one another in a way that unless you sit down and do the interviews and do the things that we've done you don't know that some of these people's relatives and ancestors are descendents of the people that owned these cabins or went to that church. Their families lived in and around these places and that to me is just remarkable. It's not a famous event that took place in that spot necessarily, you know? It's just everyday people living their lives and because of certain events in a family or in the town's history these things seem to occur."

JJ: "These haunts, I don't know if they're intelligent or not in every case, but some of them obviously are. You know, the ones that can respond, but you know also seem like they're shy because you get too many people in an area and nothing happens. When we're going to spend a couple nights in a row, the first night is relaxed. It's just kind of a bunch of people getting together making things as natural as possible, just like a bunch of tourists would do to see how the environment reacts with the people. Based on that, the second night [the night of the formal investigation] is a bit more disciplined in that you break-up into groups — each group takes their location for a certain amount of time, you take breaks so you don't get tired and crabby and then you rotate."

~~~~~

Earlier that afternoon I met Jimmy, Sandy, JJ, Chrissy, and several other team members for what would turn into a twelve-hour investigation. It seemed that the whole town knew that the 'ghost hunters' were at the old jail to uncover its phantom secrets, and a very noticeable buzz was in the air. Local newspaper reporters were on-site to interview the team members and Sandy eager to get a first-hand view into the workings of a real-live paranormal investigation. Sandy was excited and maybe even a bit nervous about what Jimmy and the team would or wouldn't find. While Sandy might have jumped at the sound of a creak or odd rapping noise, Jimmy was quick to look for the obvious explanation to the odd sound or two. As JJ mentioned, we rotated quite a bit. I joined various small teams of three to five people to investigate for a period of time in the jail, the church, and the two cabins and regularly returned to the warmth and well-lit interior of the Bass Wing to recharge with a cup of delicious Mexican hot chocolate prepared by Sandy.

My first stop of the night was the jail. I waited in total darkness with Jimmy, our voice recorders running in the downstairs room that Sandy and others had reported seeing the lights mysteriously turn on by themselves. As with other visits I'd made to supposedly haunted locations, the EVP session was exciting so long as your definition of exciting equals two relative strangers standing in a dark room at night asking questions to an empty room. The jail was not nearly as I'd expected it to look on the inside. It was fairly empty save some old display cases stored there. The museum had setup a original old ball and chain used to attach to prisoners' ankles as well as an old single bathtub all prisoners shared in hopes that the presence of these original items might provoke a reaction within the environment (i.e. prompt any lingering spirits or residual haunting phenomena to set-off) that evening. An old piano sat in the room, covered with dust, and a large, unsettling painting of an angel on the wall watched over us.

I tapped two out-of-tune keys rapidly at the far right of the keyboard.

"They hate this. I like to torture them," I said in my best Bill Murray impression. Jimmy laughed and then the silence resumed. I sat my flashlight down on the floor and asked for anyone (aside from Jimmy) in the room to turn the light on for us as a sign that we were not alone.

Suddenly, there was a distinct, low growling sound that emanated from the dark corner to my right. I froze, listening intently.

"Note, that was Jimmy's stomach," Jimmy said with a chuckle into his voice recorder.

Jimmy and I went upstairs to investigate further. It was a dark, quiet place and all of the cells had long since been removed. I snapped photos over my shoulder in the hopes of catching a glimpse of anything (or anybody) that might be silently following us as we made our way room to room. The jail wasn't the nicest looking of places, but I didn't really get any feeling of dread or impending doom exploring its innards despite its imposing exterior. As we left, I felt the growing suspicion that I would once again be disappointed with another location seemingly bereft of any ghostly activity.

Later I investigated the log cabins with JJ and a few other team members again asking questions, running K2 meters around antique tables and chairs, snapping photos in the dark, carefully minding to always say 'flash' just prior to ensure no team members were blinded by the camera. While we picked up some odd K2 readings surrounding an old table in the Carter Log House, it was not clear whether the readings came from a spook waiting in the wings or some naturally-occurring phenomena tied to the various metal artifacts (i.e. plates, flatware, etc.) lying on the table.

As we walked across to the Potter-Watson Log Cabin, the night air chilled me to the core. Stepping into the cabin the group surrounded an old teacher's desk. Sandy had indicated that this cabin had been the scene of the tragic death of a woman that fell onto an open fire earlier years ago. JJ set her K2 meter out on the table and began asking questions, attempting to start a conversation with any spirits that may have been in the room with us.

"If you're here with us we'd like to speak with you. This light sitting on the desk you can manipulate, you should be able to make the lights flicker on if you get close to it and speak. Is there anyone here with us?" JJ asked aloud.

Suddenly the meter sprang to life — three solid lights lit up and then promptly vanished!

"Is there anyone that would like to talk to us?" JJ questioned as the group fell silent quickly, all turning their attention towards the table.

Again, three lights blazed to life for several seconds and then vanished.

"Thank you. Are you female?" JJ asked.

Like clockwork, three little lights lit up a bright green and orange glow on the desk.

"Thank you. Did you live here?"

The meter sat still, the room silent.

"Did you know a woman that used to live here?" JJ asked.

No reply was given, and after several additional questions the group slowly proceeded out and back to the museum. It was strange, I'd seen a K2 meter light up at the Catfish Plantation before, but that was in a person's hands in a modernized building with full electricity running throughout. These K2 readings were from a meter sitting on a wooden desk in an empty log cabin, and while there was a lone old fluorescent light hanging above it was certainly not turned on. JJ had asked several questions before and received no response and it was a little strange that the meter reacted the way it did to three specific questions in a row. I was curious about what the cause could have been but not convinced it was the presence of a ghost.

After warming up in the museum for a bit in order to feel my fingers and toes once again, Chrissy and I made our way over to the church. I nabbed a discarded Tri-Meter, and as we approached the steps to the front door my meter suddenly sprang to life. The church was a simple single-story wood frame building with no electricity routed to it. It was hovering at about freezing outside and we were the only two people near the entrance. My Tri-Meter was set to read local magnetic field levels and as I took my first step on the short stairs and readied to open the door the meter buried the needle to the right, indicating a strong, stable reading of a 3/High.

Chrissy and I looked at each other, our eyebrows raised. Skeptical, we held flashlights and our cell phones closer to the meter trying to mess around with whatever might be the source of the reading, but still the meter persisted unchanged despite our field-testing on a solid reading of 3.

We opened the tightly shut door and entered into the church. Chrissy asked aloud if anyone was present with us. The darkened church had a foreboding appearance to it that night. The amorphous shadows hovering around the empty wooden pews were just the slightest bit disconcerting to me. As a Christian, it felt just a little uncomfortable for me to be in an old church looking for disembodied spirits. The meter in my hand continued to have the needle locked to a high reading of a nearby magnetic field.

"Is anyone here with us? If so, can you make a sound? Can you let us know you are here? We can't see you, but we may be able to hear you if you can make a sound," Chrissy said.

Without warning my Tri-Meter 'died.' The strong reading we'd been recording for several minutes disappeared suddenly and the magnetic reading dropped straight to zero. Perplexed, I handed the meter to Chrissy, who spent the rest of the session snapping photos and following sudden traces of "high" readings as they appeared in pockets around the church for the next hour or so. We were joined by others on the team including Jimmy at one point, but we were unable to determine a cause for the sporadic magnetic field readings in the forlorn church.

Later, as the group warmed up in the Bass Wing, we tested checking e-mail on our cell phones and found that it was more than plausible that the sporadic spikes we read could be attributed more to AT&T signals than those from beyond the grave. It was still interesting: why did the phones disturb the meter at some times but not others? Why would the readings persist and then vanish for long periods of time with a phone next to it or not? That we could not disprove some readings or recreate them at other times was frustrating. To my mind the verdict was still out, but if I were pressed to provide a reasonable explanation, I would have to defer to the possibility that modern technology was the root cause of at least some of our readings that night.

As the witching hour passed, the numbers of the team dwindled, as the majority of folks left for a nearby hotel. By 2 a.m., only Sandy, Andy, Jimmy, and Wes (another team member) remained. I hadn't seen or heard anything that night that overwhelmed me. I had to admit, I'd never seen the types of K2 and EMF readings I'd witnessed in the cabin and church ever before. However, I also had to admit to myself that, to Ben Radford's point, I really had no idea how my EMF meter worked or even if what it displayed as readings could be construed as evidence of a framiss. To be painfully honest, I wasn't even certain what a ghost let alone a 'type' of ghost really was in the first place for sure. Stubbornly, I vowed to myself to learn more about the possible sway my own cell phone had over electromagnetic fields and pondered whether my cell phone was potentially a serious health risk!

There we sat, Sandy on the slick slab floor next to the front door and Andy next to her. Wes was on his back, hands resting on his chest on a bright blue sleeping bag out like a light. Jimmy stood at a glass display case near the entrance typing away Facebook status updates to people following the investigation from home asking questions along the way. A personable white cat named Lulu curled up comfortably in an open antique suitcase on the floor bathing herself a few feet away as the rest of us discussed the night's events.

From the back room came a faint high-pitched sound, not unlike the sound of a bird chirp. Sandy sat up straight mid-sentence and we all stopped talking.

"Did you hear that?" Sandy asked, her head turning quickly towards the sound.

I looked over at Jimmy.

"I heard something, what did you hear?" I asked Sandy cautiously.

"I think I just heard a woman laugh," Sandy said.

I eyeballed Jimmy standing across from me and measured my words as subtly as I could. "I heard a noise, but I don't think it was a person's voice," I said.

"Oh, well I heard something," Sandy insisted.

"I did, too. I think we all did, but I don't think it was a ghost. Besides, if we did hear something didn't you say that normally it sounded like footsteps or knocks? Maybe even a man's voice whispering? If there were a ghostly voice, wouldn't it be more likely that you'd hear a man?" I offered.

"Yeah, you're right. Sorry, I'm just a little on edge still I guess. It's exciting, but maybe it's my ears playing tricks on me," Sandy admitted sheepishly.

Sandy had been a little jumpy that night for very natural reasons. It was exciting for her, what would the team find in terms of evidence following the investigation? What would it mean for the museum? Sandy wanted to believe that maybe there was more to it all than just knocks and odd sounds here and there; it would validate so much of what she and others had experienced. That said, Jimmy knew he would be doing Sandy no favors by reinforcing her opinion that she'd heard a female's ghostly laugh when he and I only heard an anonymous noise ourselves.

We continued our conversation, certain with all of the lights burning brightly and in the company of others that we were in a ghost-free zone.

"So Michael has this ongoing joke where he says 'that's what she said' each time someone says something that can be misconstrued as sexual in its tone..." I was saying when from the other room...

Ba-Ba-bah Mhn, bhn-BAH

I stopped suddenly. Sandy, Jimmy, Andy, and I were instantly alert. From the back storage room, doors open and lights on, I heard what I could only describe as two grown men's voices in mid-conversation with each other. The voices were clear, but the words were muffled.

A few tense seconds passed. All of us exchanged fevered glances. Jimmy ran his finger silently in a hurried circle motion, pressing us to keep talking as though nothing had just happened.

"So...Jan said 'Michael, I can't stay on top of you 24 hours'..." I began when...

BAH, Dah-Ghm

Again, louder than just a few moments before I heard what I could only interpret as a man's voice clear-as-day in the adjoining room. Our eyes were all wide-open as we shot looks back and forth across the small circle at each other in the main museum.

"Okay... I'm going to count to three. On three, everyone say what you thought just happened. One, two, three," I said.

In unison the four of us each said that they'd heard the sound of male voices talking in the other room. The problem was that we were all alone, we could clearly look directly into the room with all of the lights on and nobody was in there, certainly not two grown men.

I was less frightened than I was excited, my blood pumped through my veins rapidly. If what had just happened was what I thought had just happened, either all of us were having shared, sustained auditory hallucinations or I just heard the sound of phantom voices in a lit room with three strangers at 2:30 a.m. on a Sunday morning in a historical museum located in Fairfield, Texas. It was an exhilarating feeling.

Jimmy took a few quick steps with me to the back room with his voice recorder in hand. We searched the room and then even looked outside the exits for any sign of people in the area that might be the cause of the voices. Nothing appeared amiss. Whatever we'd heard appeared to have come from inside the building with us. It was clear to me that whatever I'd just experienced I had no immediate, rational explanation for. We listened intently for another hour or so, but did not hear another whispered voice again.

Since then, my mind has often revisited what happened that night. I didn't have any answers that ruled out the possibility that what I had heard was not potentially paranormal — or, at the very least, unexplainable in nature. I waited eagerly for TEXPART's findings over the next few weeks.

In the meantime, I contacted those present during the investigation to get their thoughts on just what happened that night and what had been happening at the museum since.

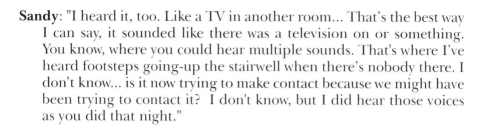

Sandy: "I heard it, too. Like a TV in another room... That's the best way I can say, it sounded like there was a television on or something. You know, where you could hear multiple sounds. That's where I've heard footsteps going-up the stairwell when there's nobody there. I don't know... is it now trying to make contact because we might have been trying to contact it? I don't know, but I did hear those voices as you did that night."

JJ: "I'm glad that you had something...a good conversation piece, shall we say, because a lot of times people will go away... I mean we lose a lot of investigators because they just get bored, they don't have anything happen."

Jimmy: "Actually that happens more often than you think that type of stuff. We may end up going back there and doing it again because we got some Class A EVPs and everything from there and some pretty interesting pictures. To be honest with you, it surprised me the quality of some of it. It's not very often you get EVPs like that and there was more than one. There was, I think, three of them over the two-day period, which was kind of remarkable. It has actually helped the museum out. People have been in there donating money. They've had a lot more foot traffic. That's really not our goal but that's one of the really good side effects of it. If it helps the museum out I'm all for it."

Sandy: "I've already had about a dozen high school kids come since the newspaper article came out...who paid to come in to see the museum and they were interested in hearing about the history, but you know why they really came, because they had read that it had paranormal activity, but I was able to kind of give them a little bit of history while they were interested in the ghost stuff, too. It's so funny because now they want to spend the night there and, people are so funny, but it has generated a lot of good things I think."

~~~~~

A few weeks later, TEXPART completed their analysis of the findings from the investigation. Jimmy went on to present the evidence gathered to the members of the board. Among the intriguing items captured were several unusual sounds/voices on tape as well as a video capturing a light switch in the downstairs area of the jail on the first night of the investigation. The light switch I'd stood right next to during my EVP session with Jimmy and it can clearly be seen to turn on by itself, springing the overhead ceiling light to life before being visibly switched off again on the wall by some unseen force. You should be able to find this clip on YouTube to view for yourself. I was confounded by the images, and that single piece of evidence made me feel all the more confident that it was one of several unusual experiences the team and myself witnessed or otherwise captured via a recording device that weekend.

I received a CD and note in the mail from Chrissy a few weeks later following a phone conversation we had regarding a possible point in the evening that Chrissy and I had following our investigation of the old church. The note read:

> Hiyas Nate,
> Thank you for the feedback about the conversation with you, Wes, and me. Because of that I am including that as a possible EVP; it will be the last one listed on the CD. I have verified with Wes also that there was nobody standing with us, and the only other possibility I had was that it was Mike. I verified with Mike and he said he was not out there.
> Several potential EVPs were listed, as was the following:
> • Night Two possible EVPs
> • The eighth one was you, Wes, and me outside the museum after leaving the Church"

I quickly opened the file on my laptop. I was prepared to hear a garbled sound, maybe a shuffling but nothing more. I asked myself 'what could be more interesting or spooky than hearing a disembodied voice in person?'

I doubled-clicked the audio file titled "Night 2 Nate_Wes_Chrissy Oh My God". The clip opened and began to play; the three of us were in mid-conversation and laughing.

> *Nate*: "Which is funny, that's what I was telling Jimmy."
> *Wes*: "We did a house that I would love to take Mike and Diane into with their DVR recorder…"
> *Nate*: "Uh-huh."
> **Male voice: "Oh my God…help me…"**
> *Wes*: "We got stuff all night long! Always where my camera wasn't."
> *Nate*: "Oh really?"
> *Wes*: "I'd move it and it would change. It's intelligent!"

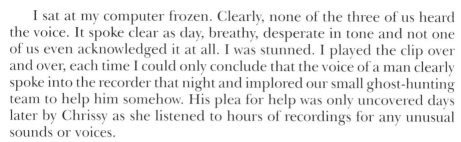

I sat at my computer frozen. Clearly, none of the three of us heard the voice. It spoke clear as day, breathy, desperate in tone and not one of us even acknowledged it at all. I was stunned. I played the clip over and over, each time I could only conclude that the voice of a man clearly spoke into the recorder that night and implored our small ghost-hunting team to help him somehow. His plea for help was only uncovered days later by Chrissy as she listened to hours of recordings for any unusual sounds or voices.

It dawned on me that what might have been most disturbing of all wasn't that I'd heard unusual voices that night, but that I might have not been listening or even able to know when a voice clearly addressed me at another point during the investigation. Could the raspy voice that emanated from my laptop speakers be that of a man who had died somewhere on the museum property years ago? Why did it sound as though the voice was desperately attempting to get the three of us to help him? Was the voice a lingering soul or something else entirely? We were outside and alone, who else could have gotten that close and why would we not have noticed? I had no easy answers to any of those questions.

~~~~~

Jimmy: "I still get spooked or startled and then you're right at it. I've seen people come into the field or join the team, we get out somewhere and something happens, they seem to be OK and then you never hear from them again. Were they not interested in this or were they not prepared for what could happen? This is something you're looking for and if something paranormal happens how are you going to handle it? Don't just scratch the surface, delve into it deeper, analyze it and really try to wrap your head around it, that goes so much further than people realize, sometimes farther than they want it to thinking about explanations for these things."

Chrissy: "I would have to say that I do not believe that there's just one kind of haunting or ghost or spirit at all. I've always believed that there's something, I just don't know what. I think that there's a lot of people fascinated by it, but they don't know where to look or they don't know where to get into it or they're going to think that their friends think that they're stupid or whatever, but I do think that there's a huge group out there. I think that there's more that do believe in it than don't believe in it."

Here in Spirit

From: Nate
To: Robin
Subject: spirit test

As for some questions for my grandparents, I thought a little bit about it and here is what I came up with:

1. Nana and Papa had a cat that lived with them (outdoor cat) when we were growing up as grandkids out at their "farm", what was its name?

2. Nana and Papa used to get together with their friend Margaret for dinner often, they had a game they usually played, what was it?

3. A cousin and I used to shoot these for target practice with a BB gun out in Nana and Papa's backyard, Nana always got upset that we'd 'waste' these, what were they?

4. When I was a boy I had a nickname for the street/road they lived on when riding down it in the car, do they remember what we all called it?

5. There used to be a field out by where my grandparents lived nearby and Papa and we would visit to walk around out in it on afternoons before a grocery store was built there. What used to be in that field that Papa liked to go look at?

Hopefully those are a few questions that they would remember the answers to. If it helps, their names are Robert (Bob) and Thelma. I really appreciate it! I'd be excited to hear from them (by way of you!) I do feel that over the years since they passed I've thought of them often and have even had a few visits from them in dreams.
Looking forward to meeting you! Thanks much. Take care!

Nate

From: Robin
To: Nate
Subject: RE: spirit test

Regarding the "spirit test," I am willing to see if your grandparents will talk to me. Please make sure that the questions are something that only you or your family knows and is not something that can be found via research. I would appreciate if you would send me the questions ahead of time so I can spend some time contacting your grandparents and hopefully they will provide the appropriate answers. It's worth a shot!

I look forward to meeting you.

Robin

"Life is something spiritual. The form may be destroyed; but the spirit remains and is living, for it is the subjective life." ~ Paracelsus (1493-1541) alchemist and physician

I didn't really believe in psychics. I thought that if there were 'real' psychics that were able to predict lotto numbers why weren't they all millionaires? I thought that 'psychic abilities' was about as specific as 'paranormal activity', a catch-all way of saying 'weird things involving the mind/supernatural' that we don't fully understand. Like ghosts, psychics have a somewhat tarnished reputation. Ghosts don't always appear on cue and psychics fail to predict horrific natural disasters that somehow even wild animals can sense coming and head for the hills to avoid destruction. People have faked ghostly photographs and some psychics have been revealed as great con artists.

Of course, there are those psychics that can supposedly talk to dead people. If ghosts are dead people roaming old buildings or desperately asking for help to everyday people that can't see or hear them then people like internationally-known psychic medium John Edward of "Crossing Over" fame must stay busy! Could it be that somehow mediums are a lot like you and I only they have some special kind of dial turned up a little louder than we do? It seemed to me that many people caught fleeting glimpses or heard the sounds of ghosts all over the world. Could it be possible that mediums have a heightened ability that they can channel for more in-depth conversations with the dead than you or I?

I asked myself this question because to this point in my search for ghosts only speculations as to what ghosts were and what they wanted had been offered to me. No one seemed to have a good reason for why these restless spirits randomly shouted out pleas for help or threw objects across the room with unseen hands. It seemed to me as though ghosts wanted different things. Could there be a ghost in Fairfield that was trying as best as he could to get my attention to help him? Did the Lady of the Lake in Dallas really just need a ride home after a boat accident? What about Frisky, the amorous ghost in San Antonio? Was he looking for a good time with sleeping female hotel guests? I didn't know the answers, but started thinking back about the idea that ghosts might retain their personalities that they had while alive. If we were but able to capture a glimpse into our world as ghosts see it and experience it, then maybe some of these random paranormal events might start to make a little more sense.

I initially contacted Robin by way of introduction by Jimmy. He hadn't always included psychics on his ghost investigations, but had invited Robin along on a few occasions and was surprised at some of the information she was able to produce about a location or the possible identity of a ghost. He suggested that I contact her to discuss her abilities further. I had a brief phone call with her to setup a meeting and sent her an e-mail outlining five questions that only myself, close family members and my deceased grandparents might know the answers to. Robin, if her psychic abilities were genuine, might be able to answer the questions. If she did, it could lend a bit of credibility to any other information she might share regarding ghosts. In the absence of any other real insight into what ghosts were and what they wanted from the rest of us with a pulse this was one of my few remaining options to try and get some answers, and maybe, just maybe know if my grandparents were still out there somewhere.

I met Robin on a cloudy February afternoon in Grapevine, Texas, at a small bistro table in the back of a bakery shop. Robin was tall, with feathery silver hair and a pretty purple blouse. She was warm, friendly and flashed a smile that made her instantly likeable and set me at ease. Aside from her usual day-to-day activities Robin led a North Texas-based website called SpiritRescueOnline.com in which one area of specialty involved fielding calls from frazzled people needing help removing ghosts from their homes. It's not every day that I met someone that held both the titles of 'Spiritual Psychic Medium' AND 'Professional Spirit Rescuer'! I wanted to hear how Robin ever got herself into those unusual fields.

"The first time that I can really remember I was about two or three years old. I had two 'imaginary friends'; my parents couldn't see them, but I played with them, I walked with them to school when I went to kindergarten and first grade. That whole time frame I spent time with them and I called them 'Lala' and 'Taki' and I found out as an adult they were my spirit guides. Taki is my master guide and Lala is actually 'Cassandra.' So they appeared to me as children when I was a child and now they're adults since I'm an adult, they kind of grew with me. They can appear any way they want to, essentially, and that's what I have found with any spirits. I've come across spirits where one moment they're a six-year-old child and the next minute they're a crone. So it's this kinda morphing thing, like 'how do I want to show you what I look like today?'" Robin said with a laugh.

"So, you were seeing these spirits from as early as you can remember. What about ghosts? Do you remember when you first started being able to contact ghosts?" I asked.

"Well, for one thing, spirits don't like to be called 'ghosts'. It's a derogatory term to them, but, yes, in my teens when I was still in high school I would see full-bodied apparitions in my bedroom doorway. It scared the crap out of me. I'd hide under the covers hoping they'd leave me alone! I didn't know what to do about it. They almost always chose to appear to me as something that was scariest to me at the moment. The movie "Carrie" had come out — one time I literally saw Carrie dripping with blood at my doorway. I now know that they can pull out what scares you and use it to get your attention, that's why I have no fear now. I can

walk into a house and they can try showing me all of this stuff and I basically kind of giggle at them. They want to get your attention," Robin said with a slight shrug of the shoulders.

"I moved out of my parent's house right when I turned eighteen and it was as if I could be myself. I didn't have to not tell everyone what I was seeing and all of this stuff. There weren't any books, the movies were all horror movies, there weren't any resources that I could find and I spent tons of time at the library trying to find something…an answer to 'what am I? Am I a witch? What am I? What is this?" Robin said.

"I always wanted to go to the oldest house in town; I always wanted to go to historic places. I'd notice the architecture, always noticing that 'oh, that doorway is new!' Well, I just saw someone walk through that doorway! That used to be a door, now it's a wall, things like that. My husband and I would walk through and I'd mention how much remodeling had been done to older places and he would ask me incredulously 'how do you know all of this stuff?' I finally had to just give him the answer that 'I have some friends that are telling me.' Somewhere along the line…they just started talking to me more…'I need help', and I kept getting these 'help' notices. I'd ask them, 'how am I supposed to help you? I don't know what to do', they would tell me that they didn't know why they were still here," Robin said.

"Wow. So what's it like? Are you just seeing people walking-by that nobody else does? Are you hearing voices? How would you describe your ability?" I asked, leaning my elbows on the table.

"It's kind of like having a radio going all the time, constantly hearing conversations. That's just one aspect, there's the seeing, the feeling, all of the other things that go with it. Basically if I had to break it down it's like having the radio on, playing in your ear all the time. I've had to learn how to block it so that I can sleep, because there was a time when I wasn't sleeping very much," Robin said with an exasperated laugh as she took a sip of her water.

"Essentially I had to say 'look, you cannot come into this space when anybody is sleeping or resting or anything like that.' That's the only way I can get some rest. It's kind of a bubble — they can't come in. I tell my guides that if the house is on fire come wake me up, otherwise leave me alone when I'm sleeping. That person has been dead for a while; they can wait until the morning. I have a phrase, 'I turn my phone off.' If anybody's going to call they'll still be dead in the morning. I have a very different view of death than most people. I do not fear it whatsoever, but most people are like 'I don't wanna die!' Like it's over," she said matter-of-factly.

"Why do you think people just don't sense these things? As a Baptist growing up I heard this idea that the other side was sort of obscured by like a thin veil people couldn't see beyond, is that somewhat accurate? Is it just our perception of the world? Can most people not see and hear these spirits?" I asked, grasping to form the right question.

"They choose not to for the most part. I believe we're all born with the abilities. It's kind of like we can all play baseball, but there are only so many all-stars, concert pianists, those kinds of things. I mean I can try, but I can't play the piano to save my life! I kind of visualize it as everybody has 'the dial'; it's whether they turn it up or not. Most people keep it off, you know, 'I don't want to listen to the music!' OK, fine. Some people, me, I don't have a choice. Dang-it! There are some days I wish I could, I'm 'on' 24/7," Robin said, her eyes glancing up and over my shoulder then back to me.

As I listened to Robin I started to get the feeling that her 'gift' might be a bit of both a blessing and a curse.

"So, let's say a person contacts you about something strange going on in their house, what is that conversation usually like?" I asked.

"People's expectations are raised because of TV and movies. When I get called into people's houses they are expecting me to be 'The Ghost Whisperer'. Sort of, but I don't stand in the town square talking out loud to spirits. TV is TV, they have to pump it up a little bit but it's not real-life," Robin said with a sigh.

"It's interesting that several of the people who have called me say 'I would never in a million years have thought I'd have a psychic medium sitting in my living room, but we have gotten to the point where this can't go on anymore.' They've called in what I call a traditional paranormal group. The group came in and took pictures, recorded audio, came back, and gave them whatever, but the spirit is still there! The client says 'that group was supposed to get rid of it', but they didn't! That's what I do!" Robin said with a laugh as she brushed a hand through her hair.

"Is it usually people's houses that are the source of the haunting activity?" I asked.

"The funny thing is that it isn't always necessarily a location. A lot of times when I get called in, one of the first things I do when I walk into somebody's house is I look around and if I see antiques I'll ask them to point out antiques that did not belong to their family. Then I have to do psychometry, which is putting my hands on it and feeling to see if somebody is attached to that and will they talk to me. A lot of the time they're attached to one of those pieces of furniture. So, don't go into antique stores!" Robin said with a big smile.

"Damn, I love antiques! That will definitely make me think twice about picking up an old clock or lamp somewhere! I want the item — not the old woman's spirit it is attached to!" I said as I laughed.

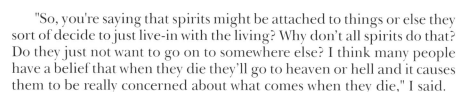

"So, you're saying that spirits might be attached to things or else they sort of decide to just live-in with the living? Why don't all spirits do that? Do they just not want to go on to somewhere else? I think many people have a belief that when they die they'll go to heaven or hell and it causes them to be really concerned about what comes when they die," I said.

"Yeah, 'am I going here or am I going there?' That's where the 'earth-bounds' come in, they don't want to go 'there'," Robin replied, as she made a frown and pointed down with her finger a few times.

"So how do they perceive things? What are spirits experiencing in these places? What's the reason for them to hang around when they should just move on?" I asked.

"The movie 'The Others' does a good job of portraying it to an extent because they think that they're living, that's probably the closest way to envision it. It's probably as frightening to them at times as it is for the living," Robin replied, glancing-up over my shoulder again briefly then back to me. I looked behind me quickly as a woman made her way back to the restroom.

"If you had a resident spirit, let's say some place says that a spirit 'lives' there, that spirit isn't always there. If the spirit is earth-bound they are acting as if it's a normal day. They may go to the grocery store, they may go to the library, and they may go to the movies! You don't know, but they're not always going to appear as full-bodied because that takes a lot of energy," Robin said, her fingers running through the back of her hair.

"So some spirits know they're dead and others don't?" I asked with uncertainty in my voice.

"Here's the question that I ask an earth-bound when they think that they are still alive. 'When was the last time you ate and when was the last time you slept?' They're like 'oh, I don't know'. I say 'well I just had breakfast this morning, I think I'm the real one'!" Robin replied.

"So it just doesn't dawn on them that they're dead?" I asked.

"They just don't have a clue because they know they still exist. I shouldn't have said that I'm the 'real' one, I'm just the 'physical' one," Robin replied, again with a look up and over my left shoulder.

"So, I guess that in a sense you could say that maybe we could all mistakenly be 'alive' in our minds as a spirit even after that 'one unfortunate accident' with the chainsaw a while back, right?" I asked, considering the possibility that some spirits might still think they are alive.

Robin had momentarily tuned me out and was again looking up and over my shoulder. I glanced behind me and didn't see anyone passing by as we sat in the back of the bistro. I smiled and turned back to Robin with a confused expression on my face.

"I'm sorry... This is going to seem really weird, but we have attracted some...people...and I keep getting poked in the head and someone's standing right here beside you. That's why I'm looking over all the time. I sort of attract spirits, especially when I visit new places. It's like I have a big neon sign over my head and they show-up to talk to me. You'll have to ask that question again, I've had to tell them all they'll need to wait their turn since I'm clearly having a conversation with you," she said with a suppressed/embarrassed laugh.

I looked back over my shoulder at the bright, empty corner of the room and imagined some invisible, impatient gentleman ghost tapping his foot on the floor wanting us to wrap up our little conversation so he could speak to Robin about things going on in his afterlife in Grapevine.

"It's sort of a series of revelations... The spirit has to have to realize that they're actually dead, especially when they claim that place is still their house. I ask them if they see the place that way and sometimes I hear from them that they kind of see things both ways at times, almost like an overlay. There's a lot of confusion on their part. When I occasionally tell them that their guide has been there trying to get them to come over to the other side they'll say 'well I'm not talking to the ghosts!' It's not something that immediately 'clicks' for them, that things are now very different," Robin said, resuming her focus on me and not the spirit poking the back of her head or standing behind me.

"Let's say some spirits do realize something is off about the world around them, when they do see people from time to time and they realize that they keep trying to get a hold of these people because they want help, is it just really frustrating for them? Are they frustrated that despite their efforts no one is noticing them? Like they're sitting in the corner yelling 'why in the hell can't you hear me?'" I asked.

"Oh yeah, exactly. That's when a traditional group comes in and starts acknowledging this activity — pictures, audio, whatever — but they don't do anything. They're not actually speaking to the spirit, or if they are and the spirit responds they aren't always hearing it. That's what I call 'stirring the pot', that's when a spirit starts getting a little more aggressive in their attempts to get noticed," Robin said.

"Is it like they feel like that is their golden chance to really have someone maybe be able to notice and acknowledge them that could help them out?" I asked, thinking back to my own experiences on the Fairfield investigation.

"Yes. They do notice that if they do more they'll get more attention, and then maybe someone will actually pay attention to them. Say that someone is suddenly remodeling what they consider to be their house.

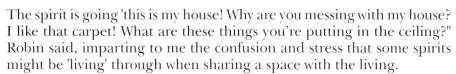

The spirit is going 'this is my house! Why are you messing with my house? I like that carpet! What are these things you're putting in the ceiling?" Robin said, imparting to me the confusion and stress that some spirits might be 'living' through when sharing a space with the living.

"Their number one motivation is 'I want to get your attention and why the heck aren't you paying attention to me?' They start by doing the little things first, but then they'll do the big things like throw something across the room to get your attention, and they'll keep escalating from that point because they realize that you notice those things, but they get frustrated because you still aren't noticing them specifically yet," Robin said with a sweeping gesture of her arm, mimicking throwing the salt shaker across the room.

"Are spirits cognizant of each other? Do they know other spirits like them are around? Some folks I spoke with at the Catfish Plantation seemed to think the spirits there might be aware of each other," I said.

"Oh yeah. There are good groups and there are bad groups. They tend to gather around each other sometimes. I've also had bad groups where one really dark spirit, one really nasty guy has found other guys that are kind of nasty but maybe not as nasty as him. He'll be like the ringleader and the four or five of them will go around and do nasty stuff. They notice that they can do all of this stuff and not get arrested, or maybe just get away with smaller stuff to amuse themselves," Robin replied.

"If people think their house is haunted, as a first step what do you suggest people do if they're concerned or frightened?" I asked.

"Don't express fear. If you have a nasty guy, he will feed on that. 'Oh, you're afraid of me, then I'll just get to poke you more', that sort of thing. What I tend to deal with are the ones that tend to be nasty. If you've got a grandmotherly spirit in the kitchen baking apple pies, or at least she thinks she's baking apple pies, that spirit is not going to bother you a whole lot unless your oven doesn't turn on or is on in the middle of the night because she's baking, but that's annoying... it's not scary so much. Depending on the living human's point of view, some people would think 'oh my gosh! My oven keeps turning on!' and get really upset. Other people would just turn it off and go back to bed. The psychology really is a big part of it," Robin replied.

"Why would a bad spirit try to scare people? What would be their motivation to do that?" I asked.

"In my experience it's more that they get a kick out of doing that stuff. Usually if it's someone in an older building, and they think it's their house they don't tend to get very nasty. My oven going on in the middle of the night wouldn't scare me, though. It depends on your perspective," Robin answered.

"So you go in to either explain to spirits that they are actually a 'ghost' and help them cross? How does that work? What if they don't want to leave and are, like you said, nasty spirits from time to time?" I asked.

"Usually I handle the spirit first and then I come back and fill in the human later. I ask clients to tell me where their 'safe room' is in their home. What room do they want to be in that they feel safe in? Pick a room they want to spend the next few hours in because I'm going to take the rest of the house. They'll ask if they can come with me and I'll always say that's up to them but generally the answer is no! They go into a room and I basically visualize a bubble over their room so they're not affected by what's going on because if a nasty spirit is going to get really nasty I don't want the client in the way. That's just for the client's safety for the most part because they don't know how to protect themselves, and I've had to learn and I make sure all of my team members are protected as well. Why do I need team members? Yes, I have my spirit guide 'buddy', but I need a physical buddy, at least one because I don't know whose house I'm walking into, they may not have the best intentions in mind for me!" Robin said. I guessed that made sense, she could be potentially walking into a haunted house or (maybe worse) the home of some deranged individual.

"If I have to go to them [the spirit], it's usually at the very minimum about three hours. It's as much education for the human clients as it is for the spirit clients in most cases. I pulled my guides in for help on how to get these spirits to move on and they said, 'All you have to do is create a door.' What? My guide said that was it, but that I had to do it because I am on this plane of existence and they're not. Well, I asked 'alright, how am I able to do that?' 'You visualize it' they said. So I basically had to learn all of this stuff myself with the help of my guides. That was tough because it really would have been nice to have had a human mentor, somebody I could call and ask for help, but it just wasn't happening. So I just started creating doors all the time and I learned very quickly that it's one-way, temporary and as soon as the door closes it erases like chalk off a chalkboard. It doesn't exist anymore. It doesn't mean that anything can come back in or anything, so I call it the 'golden door to the other side.' I basically do this little rectangle-thing with my fingers and create a door, then I tell the spirit or my guides Cassandra and Taki, usually it's one or the other is with me but if they're both there at the same time it's going to be a big day! A big day could mean that there's a large loss of life, like a major disaster today and I need to be on the call for spirits that will come to me. I tell the spirits that she'll escort them through and close the door when it's done," Robin said.

Listening to Robin she seemed to have this down to a science. I was struck by how well thought out her answers seemed to be, how easily she

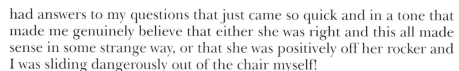

had answers to my questions that just came so quick and in a tone that made me genuinely believe that either she was right and this all made sense in some strange way, or that she was positively off her rocker and I was sliding dangerously out of the chair myself!

"The point is that these spirits are stuck and they really need to be home. They need to be on the other side…heaven, whatever you want to call it. Everybody on the spirit realm is trying to get that spirit to come over. That's where they belong, that's where we all belong, but they won't go because they won't talk to the 'ghosts.' Why? Why me? I always ask and it's because they need a human and they think they need a human to talk to. It's all based on that spirit's free will. A lot of times they are afraid of being judged somehow, some suicides for example, they think they'll go to hell. Other times they just want to stay here and play, causing problems — those are the two big ones usually," Robin said.

"So spirits are basically just people that died and either do/don't realize it, but for whatever reason just haven't made the trip back to where they belong?" I asked, trying to sum up what I'd been hearing so far.

"You are a spirit in your physical body. We all are. The difference between them and us is we still have bodies and they don't," Robin replied with a smile.

"Hmm," I said, brow furrowed.

Robin produced a folded piece of paper from her purse. She seemed to sense this was the perfect time to switch gears to something that might help me understand what she was saying in a more personal way.

"Your questions, I took some notes because it happened over a period of time. It was interesting because I was like 'can you guys just come stand here and talk to me?' They were like 'no', so it took some time," she said, referring to the five questions I had e-mailed her to ask my deceased grandparents a couple of weeks ago.

"The other side must be great for Nana and Papa, maybe it's a good thing that they are busy and have other things they'd rather be doing than answering my questions!" I said to add a little levity to whatever answers were about to come.

"They're in paradise, would you come back? They're happy; they love you and they pop in to check on you every once in a while. They'll sometimes leave little signs, smells, small items will appear, things like that," she said with that heart-lifting smile of hers.

"When they do come back, is it more for their benefit or ours?" I asked sheepishly.

"They're just checking on you. They can hear your prayers, especially if you call for them. They can hear that and be right here with you. Time and space is something we deal with, not them. If we're in Germany today it doesn't mean they couldn't show-up. They know exactly where we are.

If they've crossed-over they're happy, healthy, somewhere around the age of thirty. I don't know why, but your spirit doesn't necessarily look like you do sitting here right now, it's different looking, your appearance here is your physical body, but the spirit changes," she replied.

"Well, I don't know if you got any feedback…" I began, eager to hear what Robin found.

"I did… I have to tell you, it's not like picking up the phone and having a full-on conversation. I get impressions, I get pictures, and I hear words. Some of them mean something to them and that's a symbol that I see. The hard part for me is that I always have to be right and I know I'm not. If a psychic says to you that they're right 100% of the time, call their bluff because they're not. There's no way and here's why: the information coming in is 100% perfect, but the physical body and the interpreter are not. It's funny; I always get a kick out of things like this because it always scares the crap out of me because if I get them all wrong I'm just screwed! It's a little like Pictionary for me," Robin said, clearly a little nervous herself about how accurate her findings would be for me.

The anticipation was clearly killing us both. She began with my first question about the name of a cat (one of several through the years) that had lived with my grandparents.

"Okay, this is funny, I got two answers. The first image I got was 'Fluffy.' Now it might be that he was fluffy. The next one I got, and this was funny, this happened over multiple sessions on different days. I got 'Scat'," she said.

I pondered for a moment, not wanting to reveal anything to help Robin out in her answers in case her answers were just too broad, but also because I wanted to measure my own reactions to whatever answers she gave in an effort to make sure I wasn't reading into them too much.

"There was a big cat that lived there for a while, his name was 'Bob John' and he was a black and white cat, he was just fat and lazy! The other one's name was 'Squeaky', they named her after a squeaky screen door because of the grating meows she made, and she was a mean outdoor cat that didn't like people in general. She was the one I was thinking of in particular," I said.

"Did your grandfather ever tell the cats like, 'scat-cat, get out of here'?" Robin asked.

My heart sank. "Yeah, like 'scat-cat, get out of here', yeah…" I answered. It was odd, I hadn't thought of it in years, but Papa did seem to say 'scat cat' to get the cats to get out of the garage or off of the porch. Sure, it wasn't the name of a cat they had, but in the context of my grandparents that expression rang a bell in my memory.

"Okay, okay... Maybe that's what it came from because that was the next picture I got was someone going scat!" Robin said.

She began answering the next question. "Okay, let's see," Robin said, her eyes glancing back over her notes. "Oh their friend Margaret over for dinner..."

"I'm assuming they're Baptists so they probably didn't drink gin..." Robin started to ask.

"Not too much, maybe some Boone's Farm or Milwaukee's Best," I said with a laugh.

"Okay, because I got 'gin-rummy' or cards," she said.

Again, taking a few seconds to reflect on the answer, something dawned on me. "Rummikub, the dominoes game. You know, the colored dominoes game?" I asked Robin.

"Okay, because I wrote the 'gin' in afterwards because first I got 'rum' and I interpreted that as 'rummy' for cards. Yeah, like red, yellow, green dominoes. Interesting..." she replied, holding up her piece of paper with the word 'rum' clearly written and then scratched out with 'gin' and a question mark next to it.

I admit, the first answer was a little off, but if I were to concede that the responses Robin may have been receiving from my grandparents' spirits (who she didn't know in this life) somewhere across time and space I could maybe forgive her a bit for the shaky connection to my obscure questions. She began the third answer to my question about what the grandkids used to shoot with our Red Rider BB guns in their backyard.

"Shoot targets at these... It's funny because the first thing I got was aluminum cans, which was just too obvious, but that's because that's what I shot at. The other thing I got was like butter tubs, or plastic tubs," she said.

"Well my grandparents stockpiled cases of cans in the storage closet so we always had them. Nana would get all of these diet and caffeine-free Cokes. Well the grandkids all hated those; we loved caffeine and sugary drinks because we were kids!" I replied.

"So you shot the full ones?" Robin asked with a raised eyebrow.

"We would shake up the full ones out back and shoot them so they'd blow up. Nana was upset that we were wasting Cokes that someone else would drink. They tasted horrible, but she would see the ones that had been blown-up from the inside she could tell from the ones that were empty before we started shooting at them. Pots, we might have shot at some plant pots, but yes, cans we shot for sure," I said. Robin's head nodded-along as she began to give the answer to the nickname of the road Nana and Papa used to live on.

"Okay, the road-thing really messed with me. Essentially what I got was it was a bumpy kinda-rollercoaster kind of road," she said.

Again, I was sort of startled by her answer.

"Yeah, it was an unpaved gravel road when they moved out to Roanoke, Texas. Every time it was time to turn down that street when I was a kid my brother or I would get in the driver's lap and drive down 'bumpy road,'" I said, still a little shocked by the frank, concise way she had answered that question.

"When they told me bumpy road I thought it couldn't be 'bumpy' road. Both my father-in-law and my husband have gone by the nickname 'Bump', so I kept asking them the question, but I kept getting this bumpy, all-over-the-place, jarring-ride image like a roller-coaster and they were just adamant about it. So now I see it. They were just adamant that it was a bumpy road!" Robin replied.

"Papa used to have a tractor that he would use to go out after bad storms and smooth out the gravel in both lanes for them and all of the neighbors. It was a long, bumpy road that led to their house," I said.

"Oh, that's cool," Robin replied.

"Now it's paved over, of course. I thought if you could get that question right I'd be a little impressed!" I said, and I was impressed by Robin's answers up to that point.

"I would never have known that, and that's why I said — ask some questions that there is no way I would know or could investigate somehow," she said.

We sat there for a moment and shared a smile. The answers were going fairly well for Robin and those same answers were resonating with me and my expectations of the answers my grandparents might have given. It wasn't what I'd expected necessarily but I couldn't deny it to either Robin or myself, the majority of the answers had been unusually accurate if not outright correct so far.

"Okay, so finally the fields... What I see is when I was a little kid, I grew up directly south of LAX and when I was two or three years old they took me to the airport which is now a huge international airport but it was just a little, tiny 'nothing' airport and there was a bush bean field and I picked beans and ate them. That was the first thing; it was like the LAX property was what I kept getting. Then the other day I got wildflowers and bluebonnets," she said.

"Well if you were to drive down Southlake Boulevard heading towards Keller, Texas, there's a point where you run into Randol Mill Avenue and on the left is a shopping center today. It used to be a big open field and small airstrip. Papa used to be a pilot and loved planes of all types. It was a field with a lot of Indian Paintbrushes and other flowers in it with these aluminum port covers for little private single-prop airplanes to park. Papa used to take us out to go look into the cockpits of the planes, stand on the wings and watch the windsock blow on the runway, it was neat, a great memory I have of those times," I said.

"So it's less about the wildflowers than it was about the LAX! That's funny! See? The pictures they give me are my references," she said with a laugh.

There's no way that Robin should have known what field I was talking about, let alone that my grandparents even lived in Texas at all, or even that there was a specific field with an airport nearby that has been gone for years! She shouldn't have known that especially since I never told her that in my notes to her. Where would she have researched her answers? I asked those specific questions because if she were wrong, well, it'd be pretty clear. She could have said we used to shoot at bottles and would have been immediately wrong. She could have said 'winding road' and been completely off. She could have said that we liked to visit a field to look at the cows in it growing up, but she didn't. If she had said that my grandparent's after-dinner game was poker, it would have immediately sounded incorrect to me based on what only myself and my grandparents knew and they haven't be talking to the living recently as far as I know!

As we wrapped up, we were both a little surprised at how the Q&A session went. As I said earlier, I wasn't a big believer in psychic mediums, but I couldn't say that Robin, essentially a stranger to me, would have had a better alternative way of procuring the answers without either an advanced method of investigating my personal background online or having an advanced psychic ability that allowed her to converse with the spirit world most of us don't see or hear. In light of our little 'spirit test' and the general accuracy of the results I started to feel the weight of the rest of our conversation sinking-in. A lot of what Robin said was just so matter-of-fact, so plausible, so...well, 'common sense'-sounding that it made a potentially scary topic like ghosts seem fairly straightforward.

It made sense to me that if ghosts are just like us minus the body they might have their own motivations, some may be good, others not so much. There may be confused spirits seeking our help in some way, or at least those that want attention, that want recognition that they are still there with us. What Robin had given me was a context by which to consider what ghosts are, what they're experiencing and why they do what they do. All of these thoughts rushed to my mind, but I told Robin I was still not certain she would convince skeptics.

"The only way I think you could prove that there are actually spirits to people, because I believe that spirits are a form of energy, would be to figure-out what frequency that energy is. We just can't do that yet," she said holding her hands up in the air as if to say she didn't have all of the answers either.

As our conversation was ending, I couldn't help but think that Robin had echoed what others had said to me previously. Believers and skeptics alike acknowledged that something was certainly going on with regard to ghosts; it was exactly 'what' that was the question. Most agreed none of us would know it in our lifetimes. Yet Robin was different. She seemed to concede that while some people might not always believe her, including those that call her in a last-ditch attempt to deal with the unbelievable things taking place in their own homes, finally contacting a (gulp!) psychic medium for answers where scientific investigation had failed to remove the paranormal activity. Her perspective was unique among the others I'd heard and it was a hopeful, human perspective on something unknown and scary to most of us.

As we shook hands and departed the little bistro on Main Street I walked along the sidewalk, looking back to see Robin through the many people walking past as she was getting into her car. I was happy. I felt

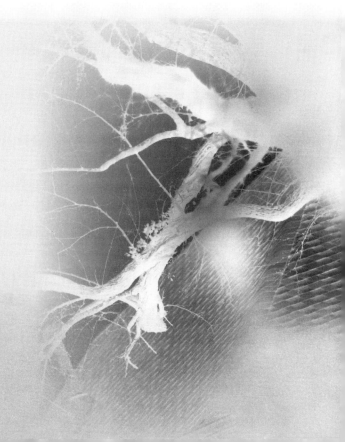

an odd renewed sense of optimism about not only my own life and my memories about my grandparents, but also about the prospect that they as well as myself and all others would eventually find our way to a place that is in some ways bigger than life and full of answers to the questions we struggle with here on Earth. I still wasn't sold on the idea of 'psychics' in general, but I had to give it to her — right, wrong or somewhere in-between — I sort of believed what she had told me and it added up in some weird way. It made those one off-encounters I'd heard about, those random spooky moments that I and the people I'd been meeting had experienced, sort of fit into a much larger picture.

I wondered if maybe we all weren't ghosts after all, spirits in bodies in life and then spirits without a body the rest of the time. I also wondered if Robin's new 'friends' from the bistro hopped in her car as she drove away, finally able to get the attention of some special person that noticed them when all others didn't.

Afterword

When we set out on our search for the ghosts of Texas, I wasn't too sure what I'd find. We met a lot of very different people, many of whom had very similar stories. There are many more places I'm itching to visit in Texas — more hotels with phantom guests, ghost lights along dark roads and more!

Originally I didn't want to persuade you folks one way or the other on ghosts. Yet as I went along I had a change of heart and did selfishly want you to do at least one thing when you set this book down: make up your own mind.

After all of this, what do I believe, you ask? I think there's something to it. We met people standing firmly on both sides of the line in the sand, separating believer from skeptic, and were able to consider several views on life and the afterlife that I don't usually find presented in a single place. Sure I don't see ghosts every day, but then again I also don't run into celebrities frequently either! I think that there is genuinely some sort of as-of-yet unexplained phenomena out there. I've met too many very different people with similar experiences to just disregard the possibility. Ghosts make life much more interesting at the very least, and I can't deny that I've had a few experiences in the course of writing this book that make me lean a little more towards the believer camp. Ghosts challenge us to wrap our brain around the possibility that there is something out there that occupies a unique place just outside our current ability to comprehend, and I doubt that will change any time soon.

I hope you've had a heck of a time joining me on my journey and I hope that it has been as fun for you as it was for me. I'll continue on in my personal search for ghosts and all the other creatures of the night that have fascinated me my entire life, and if these things interest you I encourage you to share your thoughts and ideas with others whether they share your views or not. It is only by continuing to challenge our beliefs with new experiences, new methods of investigation and analysis that we'll shed more light on ghosts in Texas or wherever else they may roam!

"Certain it is, the place still continues under the sway of some bewitching power, that holds a spell over the minds of the good people, causing them to walk in a continual reverie. They are given to all kinds of marvelous beliefs; are subject to trances and visions; and frequently see strange sights, and hear music and voices in the air. The whole neighborhood abounds with local tales, haunted spots, and twilight superstitions; stars shoot and meteors glare oftener across the valley than in any other part of the country, and the nightmare, with her whole ninefold, seems to make it the favorite scene of her gambols."

Washington Irving
The Legend of Sleepy Hollow

Index